Contents

Fast Bytes

DivX

Dr. R. Hattenhauer

DATA BECKER®

Copyright © 2001 by   DATA BECKER GmbH & Co. KG
Merowingerstr. 30
40223 Düsseldorf

Copyright © 2002 by   DATA BECKER CORP
154 Wells Avenue
Newton
MA 02459

Published by   DATA BECKER CORP
154 Wells Avenue
Newton
MA 02459

Author   Dr. Rainer Hattenhauer

Printed in the United States   Januray 2002

UPC CODE   6-80466-90207-2

ISBN #   1-58507-112-9

DATABECKER® is a registered trademark no. **2 017 966**

DivX – Compact movie theatre

After the huge success of the mp3 music compression process, a new buzzword is causing excitement on the PC scene: DivX, the new standard procedure for "shrinking" video material. The possibilities are indeed impressive.

Entire movies can be put on a standard CD-ROM, they can be of incredibly high quality, and – similar to the now widespread DVDs – they can serve as your mobile video library. The expenses for the required hardware (standard CD burner + CD-ROM) are a fraction of the estimated expenses for creating a DVD with the same image quality.

PCs can now also be used as digital video recorders by means of an inexpensive TV card. Because of DivX coding, the incidental flood of data can be reduced during the recording process and temporarily saved in a space-efficient manner on the hard drive. Any interfering commercials or channel logos can be removed afterwards so that you can fully enjoy your movie.

Whether it is a short video about the new addition to the family or a new movie trailer, nothing stands in the way now of exchanging private or published film material over the Internet. If you use a simple modem, a one-minute long DivX movie of medium quality can be transferred within the same time period (that is, within one minute).

If you think this is only possible if you have technical expertise, expensive software, and a top-class computer, you are mistaken.

The instructions herein enable you to reproduce the previously mentioned examples step by step (provided average hardware equipment is available to you) and to produce your own DivX material in no time. Take an active part in the digital video revolution!

1. Backup copies of DVDs – One click and that's it!

Anybody who ever experienced expensive DVDs being used as coasters and made unusable by scratches during a movie night ardently wishes to possess at least one copy of the expensive media. Creating such a copy is legitimate if you own the original (see below). The extraction of a trailer is used as an example. Of course, you can use the same procedure to put your favorite scenes from one or even from several movies onto CD-ROM. The chapter *Saving space for the essential* illustrates how to copy an entire movie to a single CD by applying a few tricks, so you can use your copies for the next movie night.

Attention: Copying DVDs

You must fully understand that it is only legitimate to create excerpts or copies of your DVDs if you are the legal owner. Also pay attention that some manufacturers might not allow any duplication of their media.

The "DivX" codec

The basic requirement of all DivX coding procedures is the installation of the DivX codec on your PC.

Information: What is a codec?

A codec is software used for **co**ding and **de**coding of audio or video material – most of the time to reduce the file size (as in our case).

The DivX codec was used for all of the procedures explained in this book. Go to http://www.divx.com to conveniently download it from the Internet. Download the entire DivX bundle, which already contains the player – also known as *The Playa* – which is needed to playback DivX movies. Otherwise, you might only be updating the codec.

1. Backup copies of DVDs – One click and that's it!

After the download, the program illustrated here is saved on your hard drive.

DivX4FullInstaller

The actual installation, which might be familiar to you from other Windows programs, is started by double-clicking the icon. To check if the codec was set up correctly in your system, open the Device Manager (right-click *My Computer* on your desktop and select *Properties/Hardware/Device Manager*).

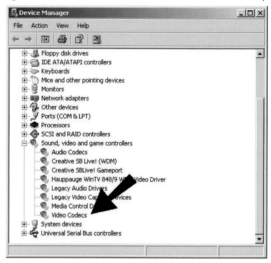

Open the *Sound, video and game controllers* category and double-click the entry *Video Codecs*. Then select the *Properties* tab. You should find the entry *DivX* with its current version number there. And voilà – the basic requirement for the coding process has been met!

"Ripping" DVDs

Let's get to the tricky part of our toolbox. Insert a DVD in your DVD drive and examine it using Windows Explorer. Note the two directories AUDIO_TS and VIDEO_TS. VIDEO_TS is the directory that is of interest.

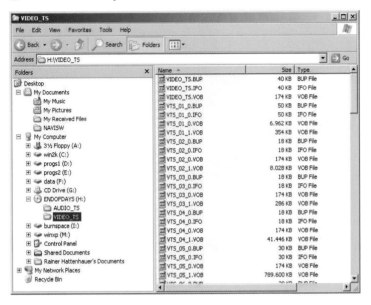

Try to drag a VOB file to your hard drive (to "rip" it). Some DVDs even allow you to do that without an error message being displayed. If this works in your case, you can check if the copied file can be played back with a software DVD player in *File* mode (see arrow in illustration).

1. Backup copies of DVDs – One click and that's it!

You receive a nasty surprise …

The reason for this unpleasant sight is the understandable desire of DVD manufacturers to scramble DVDs by using CSS (Content Scrambling System) to stop all copying attempts. Don't give up, however. It was only a question of time before resourceful programmers found a way to annul this protective measure by using a counteragent called De-CSS.

 Attention: Gray area

Note again that any further instructions explicitly refer to the copying of DVDs that are already your **property**. The author and publisher dissociate from any illegal copying of DVDs that are not your personal property.

Over time, the original spare De-CSS evolved to graphic interfaces that make the extraction of VOBs easy. One of these programs is *SmartRipper*.

 SmartRipper: Where do I get it?

Because of the dynamics of these programs, it is advisable to look for the corresponding link by using a current search engine.

The following instructions are based on the assumption that you have passed your Internet driver's license and found the above-mentioned program. Insert a DVD in your drive and start SmartRipper by clicking the program icon. Immediately after the program starts, it reads the DVD and displays the following image:

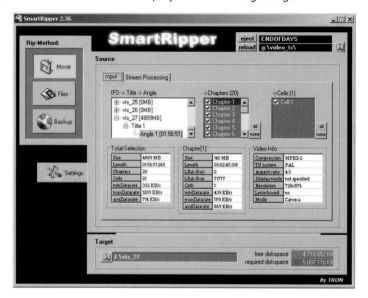

The program's structure is pretty self-explanatory.

By default, SmartRipper starts in the *Movie* mode that allows you to select individual chapters of the movie (as you are already familiar with from your DVD player). The *Files* mode allows you to selectively choose VOB files. The *Backup* mode – you've guessed it – allows you to transfer the entire DVD to your hard drive.

As a first test, rip an individual chapter of a DVD. How do you know, however, which is the desired chapter?

Assigning chapters with a software DVD player

The easiest way to identify movie chapters inserted in a software DVD player is by their identifiers on the panel. In the illustration below, for instance, chapter 3 of title 27 (which corresponds to the VOB file number) was selected.

Note

1. Backup copies of DVDs – One click and that's it!

Switch Smartripper to *Movie* mode now.

1 The program automatically selects all chapters of the largest VOB file (here No. 27). Clear the already selected chapters (here No. 3) by clicking *none*. If previously there wasn't enough disk space for carrying out the ripping procedure (recognizable from the *free diskspace* data), the required space has been freed up now.

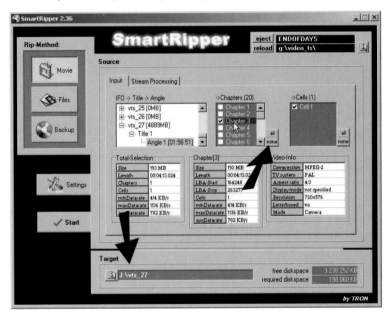

2 Look for the chapter that interests you and select it. A new *Start* button should be displayed, which starts the actual ripping process later on. Click Explorer to define the desired target directory and the name of the target file. All other settings are not of interest to you for now.

3 Click Start to extract the VOB file.

If you open the ripped chapter in the software DVD player again, the result is more pleasant this time.

Using Vidomi to create your DivX movie

The next program enables you to convert a DVD file to a DivX file (that is, to encode it) in a simple manner, with virtually one mouse click. The program is called *Vidomi;* it's freeware and can be downloaded from http://www.vidomi.com.

vidomi372

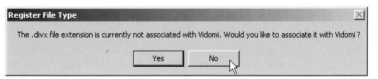

Obtain a self-installing program. The DivX codec is usually installed automatically during the setup. Download the most up-to-date version (as explained above) from http://www.divx.com. You need to take a few things into account:

1 Double-click the program icon to start the installation. Confirm the displayed license agreement by clicking *Next.* A window containing the installation options opens. Remove the check mark in front of *Install Divx* by clicking it. This way the original codec is preserved.

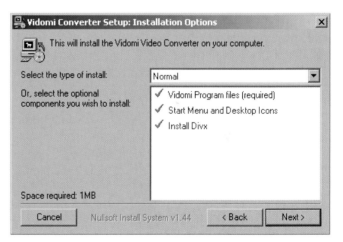

2 Enter the desired program file path in the next dialog window and confirm your selection.

1. Backup copies of DVDs - One click and that's it!

3 You are asked if files with the extension *.divx should always be associated with Vidomi. Click *No* because *The Playa* should be used to open these files in the future.

4 The program starts in *Player* mode and tries to establish an Internet connection to look for program updates. Because this feature might be annoying on a continuing basis, you can disable the auto update mode as follows:

5 In *Player* mode, open the *Mode* menu and select the *Encoder* mode.

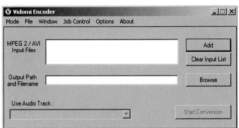

6 Now select *Options > General Options*. Remove the check mark in front of *Check For New Versions*. In addition, it can be useful to change the *File Extension* option to *.avi as some software DivX players cannot do anything with the file extension *.divx.

From DVD to DivX movie ...

In this section, you move closer to your goal of creating a backup copy of a DVD movie step by step. As already mentioned above, you limit yourself to the ripping and encoding of trailers. You can copy an entire movie without any problems afterwards. To achieve optimum results, you must take additional techniques into account, which are explained in the chapter *Reserving space for the essential*.

1 Insert your favorite DVD and start *SmartRipper*. It is advisable to use the *Files* mode for a trailer. Clear all of the selected files by clicking *none*. The VOB file of the trailer is usually a few tens of MB in size (in this example, 41.4 MB). As explained above, the software DVD player aids you in finding the desired file.

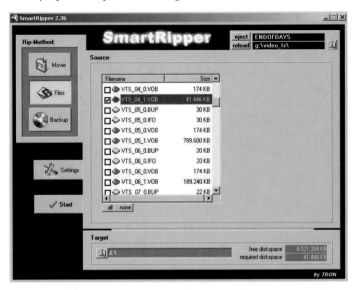

2 Start the ripping process by clicking *Start*. A progress window appears that informs you about the partial file currently being ripped (*Position*) and the overall ripping progress (*Progress*).

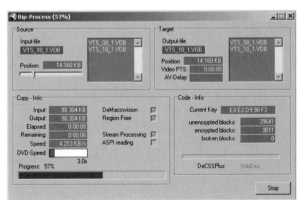

1. Backup copies of DVDs – One click and that's it!

3 Test the trailer in the software DVD player.

4 Assume that your trailer is located in the target directory of your choice. Start *Vidomi* and switch to *Encoder* mode. The program should still be in this mode from the last time you opened it. Click *Add*. A browser window opens in which you can conveniently define your VOB file. Enter the name and location of the target file in the *Output Path* data entry field.

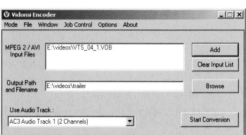

5 Now let the program know that the movie should be encoded in DivX. Open the *Options* menu and select the option *Video Options*. The dialog window illustrated here appears. The number of parameters might seem confusing. Leave the default settings the way they are and click *Select Video Codec Defaults*.

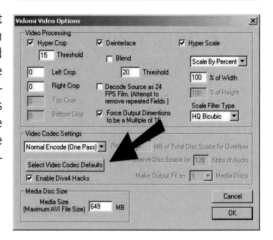

6 You come to the crucial part now. Select the DivX codec to be your compressor and confirm your selection with *OK*. You don't have to worry about *Configure* right now because you return to it in the *Fine-tuning* chapter. Click *OK* to close the *Video Options* dialog window.

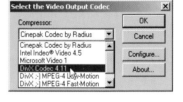

7 Click *Start Conversion* and the conversion to DivX format begins. You can view the part of the movie currently converted in an additional window. As you might notice, this process is dependent on the processing speed of your computer and might take some time.

Night-time is the encoder's best friend

It is a good idea to encode entire movies overnight as your computer has nothing better to do at that time. Even if you use up-to-date multi-tasking operating systems such as Windows 2000/XP, your processor operates at full capacity during the encoding process. Consequently, any other programs are running slowly in the background – unless you own a supercomputer.

8 Now it's time to harvest the fruit of your labor. You can use *Windows Media Player* and of course the DivX *Playa* to view the trailer. After the standard installation, (double-) click the file in the window (for example, in Explorer) to open *The Playa* immediately. Then enjoy your first encoded trailer.

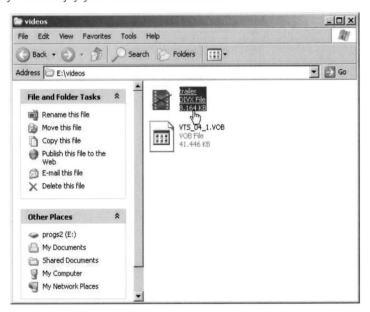

Vidomi and company

The program *Vidomi,* which was used here, is an all-in-one solution and is intended for the novice. Many other programs are better equipped to bring out the best in a movie – especially to optimizie the file size. With regard to optimizing (*Fine-tuning* chapter), programs such as *NanDub,* for instance, can only be covered to a limited extent, as explanations of every possible parameter of this program would go beyond the scope of this book.

DVDx – The "one-click solution"

Most likely you have asked yourself already, "Isn't there an easier way, for instance, a one-click solution"?

There is! The program is called DVDx. It allows you to copy an entire DVD with one click.

Download address for DVDx

You can download the freeware program from http://www2.labdv.com/dvdx

The program has limited configuration options, however. Particularly individual chapters or trailers can be encoded only by taking a detour and using SmartRipper – and it's still somewhat easier in conjunction with Vidomi.

Nevertheless, you can enjoy a "one-click copy" by following the following instructions.

1 Start DVDx and select the menu item *Open DVD root*. The *Select Title* dialog window should appear. If it does not, you must use the integrated Explorer to get to the DVD video directory.

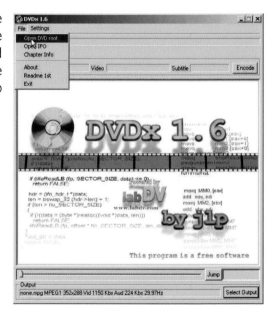

2 Select the longest program from the list of titles and confirm your selection with *OK*.

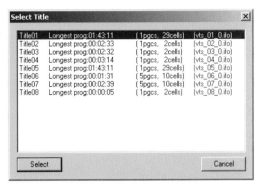

3 Select the English audio track in the *Input setting* dialog window and check the option *Audio/Video synchronisation*. You can enable or disable the display of subtitles as desired. Leave the remaining settings unchanged and confirm your selection with *OK*. Then view the movie and its possible subtitles in the preview window. Click *Select Output* to define an output file.

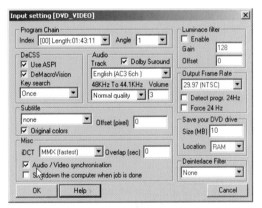

4 As displayed in the illustration below, define DivX and mp3 as your video and audio codecs. **Very important:** Click *Whole*; otherwise, only the minimum number of frames and not the entire movie is encoded. You can leave the resolution at the default values of 384x240. Confirm your settings by clicking *Apply*.

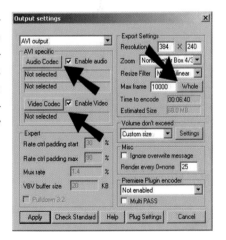

1. Backup copies of DVDs – One click and that's it!

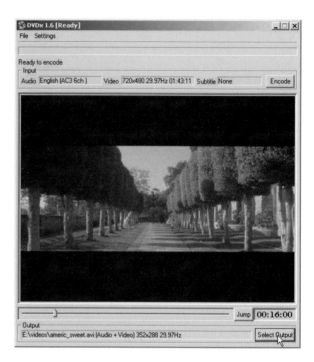

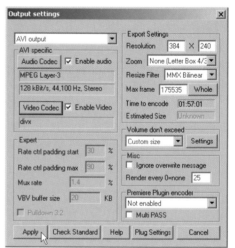

5 Use the slider in the main window to go to the beginning of the movie. Click *Encode* and the "one-click conversion" begins. You can track the encoding process directly in the preview window. For control purposes, you can stop the encoding process by clicking *Stop* and view the DivX file in the player. You can also encode sections from the center of the movie by using the slider to select the corresponding positions.

Like many of the currently available "one-click solutions", the program is very convenient; however, it offers less flexibility than the SmartRipper/Vidomi solution.

More extensive configuration option ...

... are offered by another one-click tool: EasyDivX

EasyDivX represents an integrated solution. As with DVDx, it only takes a mouse click for the conversion to take place. The configuration is more difficult, however, as you must know the effect of each program parameter. On the other hand, the program offers more fine-tuning options.

You can download the program from http://easydivx.does.it.

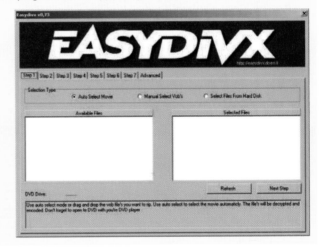

2. Your computer as a digital video recorder

The term "*video on demand*" – that is, having access to digital videos whenever and wherever you want – is certainly a major catch phrase of this media age. Who doesn't dream of archiving favorite TV shows and TV series inexpensively and digitally in order to have them ready when needed, like the audio CDs of your CD collection.

The next chapter demonstrates step by step how you can implement this project cost-effectively. For this purpose, you only need a computer of medium quality (Pentium III 500, 128 MB Memory, approx. 5 MB free disk space) as well as a TV card (starting at $65.00 in specialized stores). If your graphics card offers *Video In*, you can save yourself the latter investment.

You can even download the software for free from the Internet. You use the freeware VirtualDub, which is an amazing digital video editing program.

VirtualDub on the Net

You can find VirtualDub on the following Web site: http://www.virtualdub.org.

If you would like to get in-depth information about the program, you can find comprehensive explanations and tutorials on this Web site.

Preparing your PC

In the following, we will limit ourselves to instructions on how to connect a standard PCI TV card. If you have a graphics card with *Video In*, you can easily apply the following steps to your system once you have identified the *Video In* with the aid of this manual.

Getting a clear TV image with your computer

Information: Optimum input of the TV signal

In contrast to TV card manufacturers, manufacturers of graphics cards have often treated Video In hardware as second class. On the other hand, the TV tuner chips of commercially available TV cards provide unsatisfactory video signals. The best solution is to use the tuner of your TV or VCR and enter the TV signal directly into the Video In of the TV card by using an adapter.

Take a look at the following illustration to get a better overview of the required wiring:

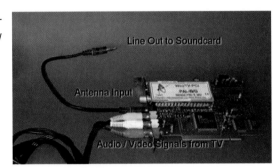

The video signal from the TV or VCR is picked up by the video adapter and then split between three Cinch connectors. The three signals (yellow = video signal, red = stereo left, white = stereo right) are directly fed into the TV card through a connecting cable. Alternatively, you could, of course, channel only the antenna signal into the TV tuner of the TV card; however, this most likely leads to a loss in quality. In addition, it is important to connect the *Line Out* of your TV card with the *Line In* of your soundcard in order to transmit the sound.

Information: Further reading

Additional helpful suggestions about the wiring of other hardware constellations can be found in the book *From VHS to DVD – The inside Angle to Digital Video* published by DATA BECKER.

Now it's time to test and adjust the TV reception on your PC, if needed, by using *VirtualDub*.

2. Your computer as a digital video recorder

Recording with VirtualDub

1 Start *VirtualDub*. Select the menu item *Capture AVI* from the *File* menu.

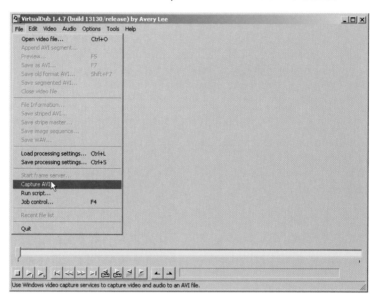

2 If you did the wiring correctly, you should now see a small TV image:

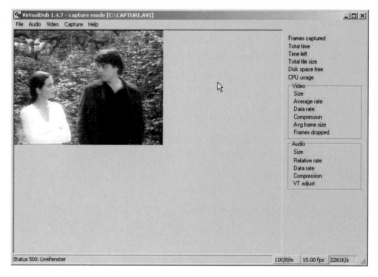

3 If, contrary to all expectations, you only see a blue area in *VirtualDub,* go to *Video/Video Source* and check if *Video Composite* was selected under *Video Connector.* If you feed in the signal through an antenna input contrary to the above explanations, select the option *Video Tuner.*

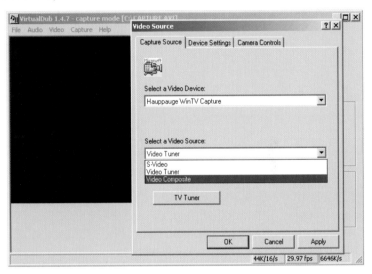

The last obstacle is to prepare the audio recording. Many novices wonder why their recordings remain without sound. Solve this problem as follows:

Preparing the audio recording

1 In *Capture* mode, open the menu *Audio/Volume Meter.* The volume level (meter) illustrated here should appear. If this is not the case:

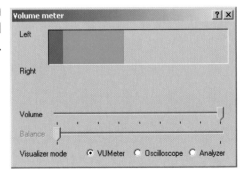

2. Your computer as a digital video recorder

2 Double-click the speaker icon in the Windows taskbar. The *Play Control* dialog window opens. Go to *Options/Properties*. Another dialog window opens that allows you to define the capture/playback settings individually. Select *Capture* and click *OK*.

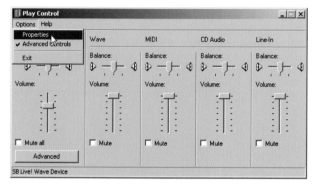

3 Ensure that *Line-In* is checked off and the volume control is set at half. Simply take a look at the *Volume Meter of VirtualDub*. The other controls should be set at zero. Otherwise, Windows selects the microphone to be the default recording source.

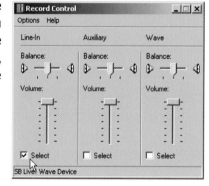

Note

Preventing distorted audio recording

If you notice later on that the audio recording is distorted during dynamic audio sections, the audio is maxed out. In this case, slide down the Line-In volume control. This should solve the problem.

Everything is working now? Great! Now you can attend to your first recording.

Camera, action!

The *on-the-fly* recording technique explained in the following section is geared towards owners of "middle-weight" computer equipment (min. PIII/500; 128 MB RAM). The section *Slow computers/fast computers* illustrates which measures have to be taken to achieve optimal recordings if weaker hardware is used. In addition, the same section offers a glimpse at the possibilities of supercomputers.

Note

On-the-fly recording ...

... means that the video material is encoded already during the recording process. The advantage of this procedure is the reduction of the amount of data that needs to be saved during the recording.

The following table offers the file sizes of a number of prominent codecs as well as of uncompressed material for a one-minute movie sequence for comparison. The resolution of the recording was set at 384x240 for each of the files.

Codec	File size
uncompressed RGB	328 MB
Huffyuv v2.1.1	244 MB
MJPEG	60 MB
DivX 4.11/1500 kbps, uncompressed audio	21 MB

If you are not planning to buy an additional hard drive for your video sequences, DivX is your method of choice. Let the fun begin!

1 Start *VirtualDub* and switch to *Capture* mode. Then go to *File/Set capture file* (or press the F2 key) to define the capture file. This step is essential, as the program (or at least older versions of it) creates an empty file if no capture file is set.

2. Your computer as a digital video recorder

2 Go to *Audio/Compression* to select the audio compression procedure. Select *CD Quality*, which is a predefined compression scheme of the program.

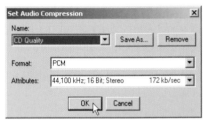

3 In the *Video Format* dialog window, select a resolution of *384x240* and the image format YUY2. Higher resolutions might require better hardware and a few tricks that are explained further in the chapter *Visual material of near-DVD quality*.

4 Go to *Video/Compression* to select the codec (in this case select DivX). Click *Configure* to open the codec configuration dialog window.

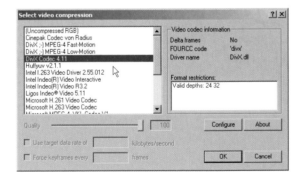

5 Set the *Variable bitrate mode* to *1-pass quality-based*. Under *Performance/Quality*, select the option *Fastest*. This way, you ensure that slower hardware can "keep up" as well.

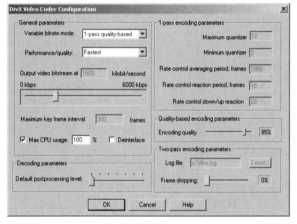

6 Go to *Capture/Settings* and set the *Frame rate* to 29.96 frames/sec, which corresponds to the NTSC standard. In addition, select *Lock video stream to audio*. This function prevents the infamous synchronization problems.

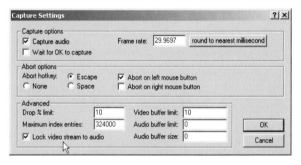

7 Save the previous settings to define starting conditions for your next capture attempts. Select all *Save* options by checking them off in the *Capture Preferences* dialog window and click *OK*.

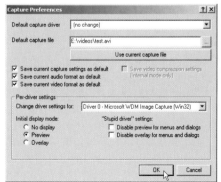

8 Here's the most important point when optimizing the system. It is essential that you open the *Video* menu and select the menu item *Preview*. This relieves the processor, and you won't exasperate yourself with the infamous *dropped frames*.

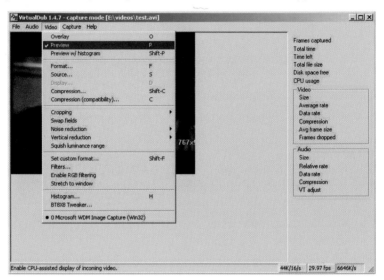

Making these settings might seem painstaking to you right now, but defining them is a lot faster the next time around. Now select *Capture Video* from the *Capture* menu (or press the F6 key) and watch how your video data is whirled onto your disk. To finish the recording, press Esc.

Attention (file) trap!

Don't forget to define the filename of the capture file first, when attempting your next capture. Otherwise, you produce the most boring movie in the world – namely "nothing".

Viewing and editing the material

Of course you want to view your first movie after capturing it on hard disk. For a first assessment of the material, use the Viewer, which is integrated in VirtualDub. Exit the *Capture* mode by going to *File/Exit capture mode*. Then, open your captured video by selecting the command *Open video file* from the *File* menu. Two empty frames are displayed. Click one of the two *Play* buttons (see arrow) at the bottom left of the program window to start the video.

The left window plays back the original video, whereas the right window plays back the video that was edited in VirtualDub. The different editing functions of the program are reviewed in detail below.

The first troubleshooting: No more static noises

If you can hear static noises in spoken parts of the video when playing it back in VirtualDub, give the DivX low motion codec a try (which is included in the DivX 4.01 bundle for compatibility reasons). The static noise can be traced back to your hardware, which might be too "weak". In this context, it has to be pointed out, however, that the old DivX codec is legally standing on shaky ground, because it is basically a hacked Microsoft codec. Therefore, avoid using it.

Audio post-compression

An important step the compression of material is the reduction of audio data.

Setting the tone: Audio post-compression with mp3

It is always recommended to record the audio in PCM format first and post-compress it to mp3 format later. This saves processing time during the recording and prevents *dropped frames*.

2. Your computer as a digital video recorder

1 In the following, you work in *Dub* mode (that is, the standard mode of VirtualDub). First open the video to be edited as previously explained. Because only the audio should be edited now, select the option *Direct stream copy* from the *Video* menu.

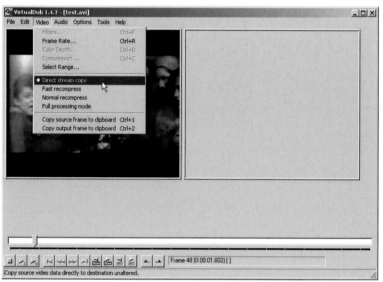

2 Select the options *Full processing mode* and *AVI audio* from the *Audio* menu. In the *Compression* window, select the option *MPEG Layer-3* as well as a bitrate of 96 kbps at 44.100 Hz/Stereo. In view of the expected size of the final file, the last selection represents the best "price/performance" ratio. Click *OK* to confirm your settings.

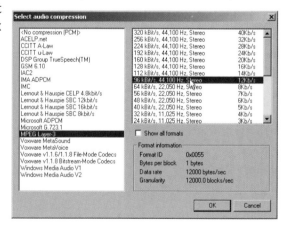

3 Save the settings that were just defined as *Processing settings* for future routine procedures. To do so, go to *File/Save processing settings* and enter a meaningful name for the settings (for example, *my_configuration*). This is particularly important if you experiment with different video settings for the purpose of optimization.

4 Now select *File/Save as AVI*, assign the post-edited video a name and confirm by clicking *OK*. The VirtualDub progress window, which is illustrated here, then appears. It informs you about the compression progress.

If you now look at the files in Explorer, the successful results of the data compression are clearly recognizable.

The file size of the video clip (which is one minute long in this case) was reduced almost to half. This result can only make us optimistic, if we think of our long-term objective (that is, placing an entire movie on one CD).

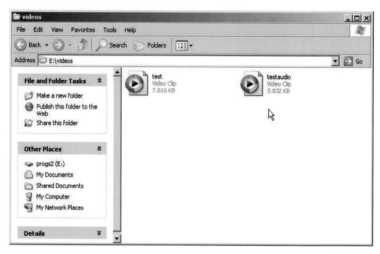

The finished video can be played back as explained in the first chapter by using *The Playa*, Windows MediaViewer or any other player of your choice.

Being in the picture: The full screen mode

With almost all of the current DivX players, you can use the keyboard shortcut Alt+ Enter to switch between full screen and regular window mode.

VirtualDub and DivX – The most important parameters

So far, you had to content yourself with following the step-by-step instructions without getting to the bottom of things by yourself; in this chapter, you can take a closer look at the software. In addition, it's good for you to experiment to make the most of your hardware.

Let's start with a few settings affecting VirtualDub itself. Select *Capture* mode first.

- **To set the stop conditions** for the video capture, go to *Capture/Stop conditions*. In the illustration, the capture stops after 60 seconds. This converts your computer into a primitive video recorder. In addition, the capture can be stopped after a certain file size is exceeded or if the free disk space drops below a certain value.

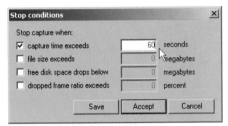

- **Cropping the capture**: *Before you start the capture,* you can use the *Video/Cropping* command to specify if a certain part of the TV image should be removed during the capture. This function is useful for removing the black borders of movies in the 16:9 format, for instance. As illustrated, the offsets are used for this purpose. This way, the amount of data being saved can be kept to a minimum already during the capture. Important: After defining the clipping area, select *Video/Cropping/Enable.*

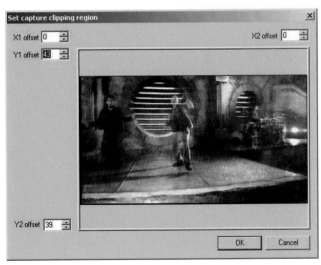

- In order to avoid **synchronization problems**, it is important to attune the audio and video data. The illustrated dialog window can be reached by going to *Capture/Timing*. Select the option *Adjust video clock to match audio clock*.

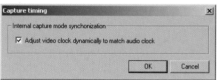

In regard to the video quality of the capture, two values intrinsically connected are of vital importance: the image resolution and the bitrate at which the DivX codec is operating.

- Go to *Video/Format...* to set a number of predefined formats. The YUY2 image format is generally to be preferred over the other formats. If you own a fast computer, you could test whether it can capture in full screen mode. More about that in the next section.

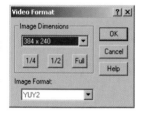

The bitrate (as well as other parameters defining the DivX codec itself) is also of utmost importance when capturing on-the-fly. Go to *Video/Compression*, select the DivX codec, and then click *Configure*. The following dialog window opens:

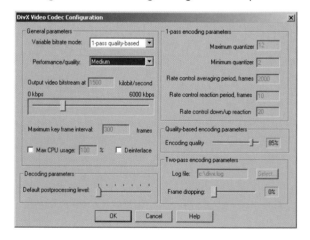

If you select the setting *1-pass quality-based*, which was chosen in the illustration, VirtualDub automatically selects the video bitrate. If the *1-pass* mode is chosen, you can define the bitrate yourself. This is an opportunity for experimentation that helps you better understand the significance of bitrate variation. Capture one minute of film at a bitrate of 1500 kbps and compare it to a film at a maximum bitrate of 6000 kbps. Compare the quality and size of the two files.

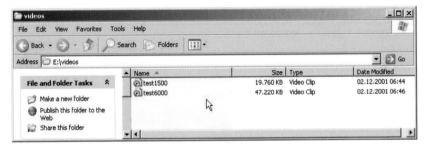

The video recorded at the higher bitrate is double in size. If you play back both videos and compare their quality, notice that the video captured at a higher bitrate is of considerably better quality.

The bitrate defines the size and quality of the video

When choosing the bitrate, it is necessary to find a compromise between the file size and quality of the video. Different bitrates also pose different demands on the hardware; your only option is to experiment to find the optimum solution for your equipment.

On the other hand, the smaller the bitrate of a captured video, the lower the hardware requirements for playing it back. This has to be considered, if you want to play the DivX video directly from the CD-ROM drive.

Slow computers/fast computers

This chapter illustrates that owners of older hardware are not excluded from using DivX technology. The minimum hardware requirements are based on a good old PII/300 MHz with 64 MB memory. The magic formula is called **Huffyuv** and is explained step by step below.

2. Your computer as a digital video recorder

The Huffyuv codec

is a codec used for almost loss-free capturing of video material. You can download the codec for free from the following Web site:

http://www.math.berkeley.edu/~benrg/Huffyuv.html

The zipped file contains the file Huffyuv.inf. By right-clicking and selecting *Install* from the pop-up menu, the codec is installed and made known to the registry.

To use Huffyuv to capture a video, proceed as follows:

1 Select the *Capture* mode of VirtualDub. Define all parameters as explained in the chapter *Camera, action!* and change the codec to Huffyuv.

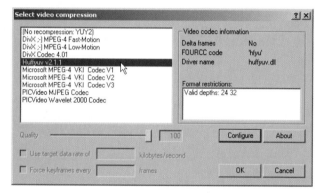

2 Ensure that you define the codec options as illustrated.

3 Confirm your settings and start by pressing F6.

Capture a one-minute video clip to test the new codec. Notice that this procedure also works with pretty outdated hardware; however, it has one flaw, as already indicated in the chapter *Camera, action!*: The resulting file size is enormous.

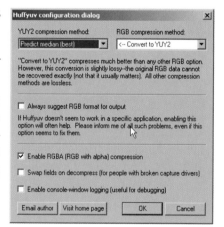

Post-compressing the raw data with the DivX codec can solve the problem. So, let's continue ...

4 Switch to the *Processing* mode of VirtualDub and open the video that was captured with Huffyuv. Make sure the menu item *Full* processing *mode* is enabled in the *Video* window. Also enable this mode in the *Audio* window.

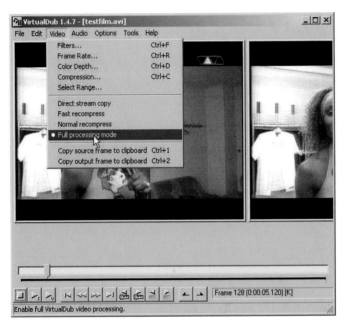

5 Go to *Video/Compression* and select DivX as your video codec, as explained above; then go to *Audio/Compression* and select mp3/128kbps for the audio compression.

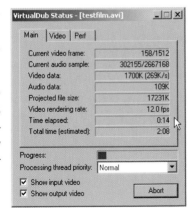

6 The actual encoding is started by going to *File/Save as avi ...* Notice that the conversion is carried out at a considerably higher video rendering rate than for on-the-fly capturing. A new analysis in Explorer show that the size of your video was reduced considerably.

Note

Why not treat yourself? The 4-GHz computer

If hardware performance is not an issue for you, you could certainly dare capture a video in full NTSC resolution (720x480). You might be confronted with another unpleasant problem, however: **interlacing**. Read more information about this subject in the *Fine-tuning* chapter.

Can I have a little bit more? The 2 GB/4 GB limit

If you are not one of the lucky computer users who own Windows 2000 or even Windows XP, you find out the hard way that "your" Windows has a problem with large files when capturing a video with the Huffyuv codec.

Note

File systems and file sizes

Two file systems are prevalent among Windows home operating systems (Windows 9x):

- The **FAT16** file system that can manage files up to a maximum size of 2 GB.
- The **FAT32** file system with which the magical limit is increased to a maximum of 4 GB.

The Windows professional operating systems Windows 2000 and Windows XP use the following file system:

- The **NTFS** file system, where the file size can be 16 Exabytes (= 17 billion GB!) – certainly an investment for the future.

But don't worry! VirtualDub does not let us down when dealing with file size problems in Win9x.

Avoiding the file size limitations

There are two parts to the solution to a limited file size. They are called *multisegment capturing* and *spill system*.

Note

Multisegment capturing:

This procedure automatically divides a video file into a number of smaller files during the video's capture.

Spill system:

If this option is enabled, VirtualDub automatically divides the captured video and distributes it to previously defined hard disk partitions.

Proceed as follows to create a spill system (consisting of two spill drives) and to multi-capture a video with the help of the Huffyuv codec (which, as already explained, creates exceptionally large file sizes). Then you learn how to merge and encode the individual files.

1 In VirtualDub, switch to *Capture* mode and go to *Capture/Capture drives*. The dialog window opens as illustrated; click *Add spill drive*.

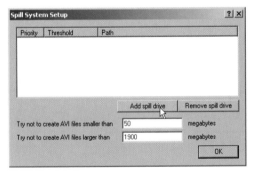

2 You can define the directory path of the desired spill drive under *Path*. Repeat this step to add further spill drives/directories to be used. Use the *Priority* function to define the priority of the spill drive. If the *Threshold* value (that is, minimum remaining free disk space) is exceeded, the next spill drive can be used.

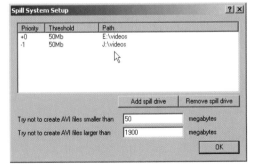

3 Now, define the maximum file size. For test purposes, select 300 MB; you should set this value to 1900 MB (FAT 16) or 3900 MB (FAT32) later on.

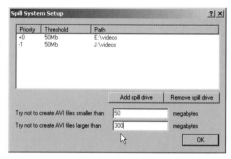

4 Important: To enable the system, select *Capture/Enable multisegment capture*.

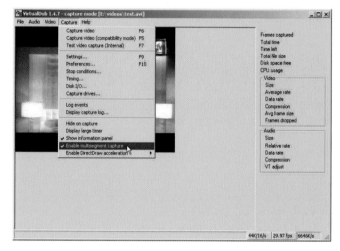

Now you can capture your video with Huffyuv as usual. The program creates file segments of the previously selected file size (in this case 300 MB). How can you merge the individual segments and encode them? It's easy.

5 In *File* mode, open the first segment of your capture (indicated by the suffix *.00). The program views all of the captured segments as a single video file, which can now be entirely encoded.

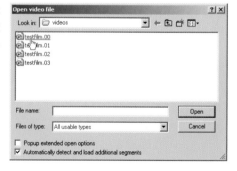

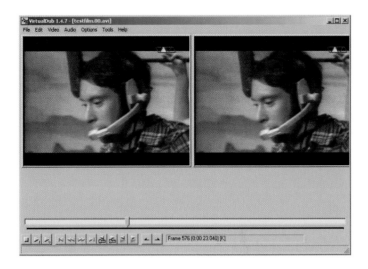

Please refer to the section *Slow computers/fast computers,* which explains the procedure of post-encoding.

Optimizing the system

> **The hard disk – The critical factor:**
>
> The above-mentioned procedures might have made one thing evident: You can never have enough hard disk space.
>
> In addition, you should make sure that the fastest possible disk/spill drive is used for the spill system. Up-to-date UATA 100 hard disks are perfect for video capturing.
>
> The best solution is to add an especially large hard disk to the UATA 100 for video purposes only.

VirtualDub even offers you a separate benchmark to test your hard disk performance. You can access the benchmark through the AuxSetup file included in the program bundle. Double-click the icon to open the following dialog window.

AuxSetup

2. Your computer as a digital video recorder

Click *Benchmark* :

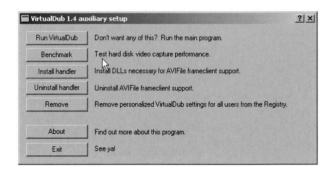

Here, you can test your hard disk and video capture performance independently. Starting the disk benchmark might yield the following results, for instance:

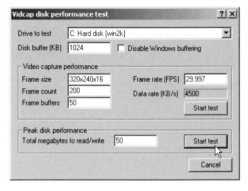

You have laid the foundation for a successful "DivX on the PC" career. In the following chapter, you can deepen your knowledge and strive to optimize your visual material.

3. Visual material of near-DVD quality – The fine-tuning

In this chapter, you learn a number of tricks for creating DivX videos of near-DVD quality. You start by optimizing the video capture and by getting to know different options for filtering the raw visual material. The chapter closes with the explanation of the different DivX codec options.

Optimized capturing: The resolution trick

You probably carried out your own experiments after following the step-by-step instructions of the previous chapters. Most likely, you had to make a compromise at one point.

For instance, you might have experienced the occurrence of *dropped frames* because a too high resolution was selected for the capturing procedure. The computer cannot process and save the flow of data at that point. Especially when you are capturing on the fly, you should take the following tip seriously.

Selecting the resolution

Note

When capturing a video, the resolution for both width and height should be a multiple of the number 16.

For **medium quality**, a resolution of **384x240** pixels is recommended.

For **high quality**, a resolution of **704x480** pixels is recommended. This format has established itself in connection with full resolution captures of NTSC video material .

The only problem is that most computers can process the 384x240 resolution but can't handle the full resolution. The solution is a golden mean obtained by a trick.

3. Visual material of near-DVD quality – The fine-tuning

1 In the *Capture mode of Vir-tualDub, proceed as follows to customize* your resolution. Go to *Video/Set custom format* (or press (Shift)+(F)) and open the *Set custom video format* dialog window. Select 384 and 480 as frame width and frame height respectively (that is, double the regular half-frame size). Define YUY2 as your data format.

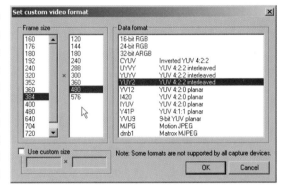

2 The preview image now appears somewhat strange, as its height has been stretched by a factor of 2. And notice something else: Stripes are displayed during fast movements. This effect is called the "comb effect", which is explained below.

Avoiding the comb effect

The comb effect results from regular TV images being displayed in half-frames that do not appear synchronized on the PC monitor. During rapid movements, the contours are blurred. You have two strategies to deal with the comb effect:

If the visual material is intended for TV, do nothing.

If the material is intended for your PC monitor, you can apply a *deinterlace filter* when editing the video in VirtualDub.

Note

For the time being, you can ignore the comb effect.

3 Now you can reduce the image vertically during the capture. Select the command *Vertical reduction* from the *Video* menu and select the option *2:1 Linear*.

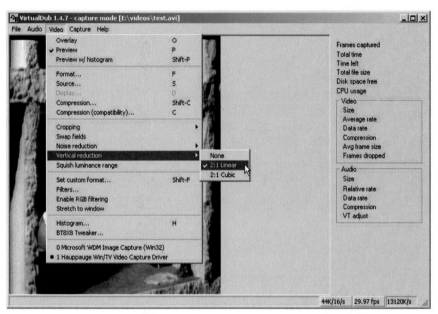

4 Now proceed as explained in the chapter *Your computer as digital video recorder* and capture the desired video sequence. (Don't forget to define the save location of the file.)

5 Open the captured file in a software DivX player of your choice. The comb effect does not occur (because of the vertical reduction), and the capture's sharp image quality is satisfying (if you compare the advertising logo of the channel with a regular capture, the improvement in quality is striking).

A video capture created this way can be between VHS and SVHS quality. If the capture is played back on TV (the chapter *DivX movies on the computer, TV, and so forth* explains how that's done), the layman might not notice a difference between a regular videotape and your copy. And isn't a small CD a lot more space-efficient than a videotape?

The Ivy League: Loss-free capturing with post-compression

It is now time to climb to the pinnacle of video compression and create highly optimized material through post-compression. Even owners of older hardware can make use of this option, for the Huffyuv coded used here burdens the processor little. The only limiting factor is the size of the hard drive, but this shouldn't be a problem in the age of the 80-GB drive. One more word of advice: Be patient when encoding.

1 In the *Set custom format* window, select the format 704x480.

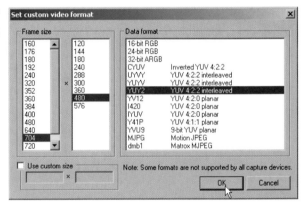

2 Use the *Huffyuv codec again* (Shift)+(C)). Leave the standard codec settings as they are.

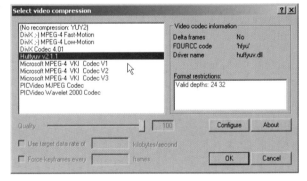

3 Now you can start capturing ((F6)). Don't be astonished if your hard drive is drowning in data. Capturing in full screen resolution can rack up about 400 MB of data for every minute of video (in the example above, a 5 GB partition can barely hold a 10-minute video), a problem which is soon to be alleviated by the constantly increasing hard drive capacities and falling hard drive prices. Yet you have other ways of obtaining optimal source material. These further options are discussed in the section *Using additional software/hardware*.

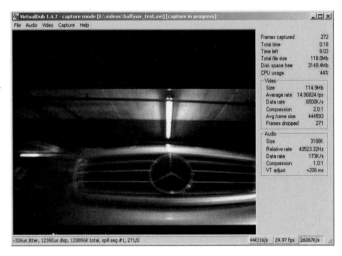

4 You have to reduce the size of the material. Quit *Capture* mode and open the file you just recorded in VirtualDub. For a better overview, *right*-click the two image sections to reduce them to half-size.

3. Visual material of near-DVD quality – The fine-tuning

5 Now, you need to determine the target resolution and the compression codec. It might be useful to select a lower target resolution for the end product to reduce the quantity of data, for instance. To meaningfully estimate the final size of the video, you should also keep in mind the bitrate you select for the codec. For more detailed information on this, see the chapter *Reserving space for the essential*. Don't change the resolution at this point, but select the DivX codec with a bitrate of 1500 kbps.

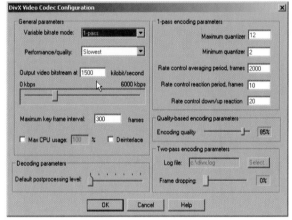

6 If you want to watch the video mainly on the computer, it is important to use a filter in the editing of the material. Go to the *Video/Filters* menu to open the adjacent window. Click *Add* to define a filter. Select the *Deinterlace* filter and confirm your selection by clicking *OK*.

7 In the window that opens, select the option Blend fields together.

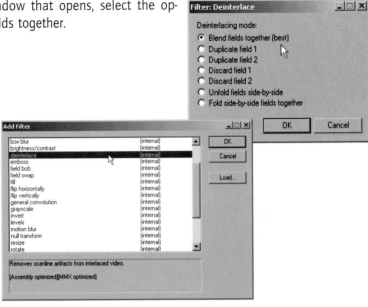

8 Now, you only need to set the audio codec to mp3/128 kbps, as described above, name the target file by going to *File/Save as AVI*, and you're done!

Save your work!

Again, you should save the settings you adjusted in VirtualDub by pressing Ctrl+S (or by going to *File/Save processing settings*). That way, you have defined a starting point for later experiments.

3. Visual material of near-DVD quality – The fine-tuning

Is the recording choppy? Lower the resolution.

Perhaps your hardware can't deal with playing the recording at full resolution. Capture Huffyuv at half-resolution and go through the steps above. In this case, you can, of course, save yourself the deinterlacing. Still, you should see an improvement in quality in comparison to on-the-fly capturing even here.

Using additional software/hardware

In this section, you are introduced to useful acquisitions with which you can substantially improve the quality of your images.

The Huge data amounts which result from capturing with Huffyuv are annoying. There should be a way to collect good-quality raw material and still save some space. The solution is the MJPEG codec.

The MJPEG codec helps reduce data

This codec is commercially available and can be downloaded from Pegasus Imaging at

http://www.jpg.com

In principle, the codec uses a *.jpeg (Joint Picture Expert Group) reduction process for motion pictures. A watermark is applied to all recordings until you register the product. You can register over the Internet for $18.

The codec is installed in a similar manner to DivX and Huffyuv. Give it a try.

Recording with MJPEG

1 *Start in Capture* mode in VirtualDub and select the full screen resolution (704x480) and MJPEG as the recording codec.

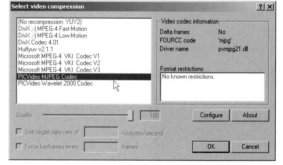

2 Click *Configure* to reach the advanced options for the codec. A compression quality of "18" should be enough for now; you'll have room for further experiments later. In this window, you can also register the codec.

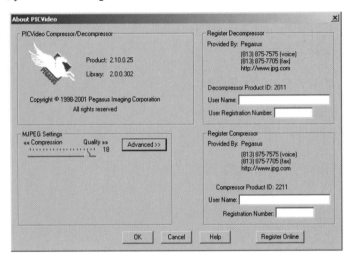

3 Capture as usual, and preview the result in Windows Media Player.

Notice that the video plays back smoothly. The picture quality, too, is outstanding in full screen mode ((Alt)+(Enter)). The image doesn't jump even if the hardware is only mid-class. The only things that distract from the enjoyment of the image are the company's watermarks, but you can get rid of them by registering the codec. One look at the file in Windows Explorer proves that the amount of data has visibly shrunk in comparison to Huffyuv.

3. Visual material of near-DVD quality – The fine-tuning

4 You can now proceed to the usual post-compression with DivX, described in the chapter *The Ivy League*. Don't forget the *Deinterlace* filter!

Check out your success using *The Playa* player, and you notice that you have climbed a little bit higher!

It doesn't always have to be full resolution

You can keep the original resolution when you encode the finished product, but that isn't necessary. Even a lower-resolution end product delivers outstanding images, especially when viewed on TV.

Lowering the resolution is simple. You need only one additional filter in VirtualDub. After defining the *Deinterlace* filter as described above, also add the *Resize filter*. *The following images illustrate the settings you need to adjust.*

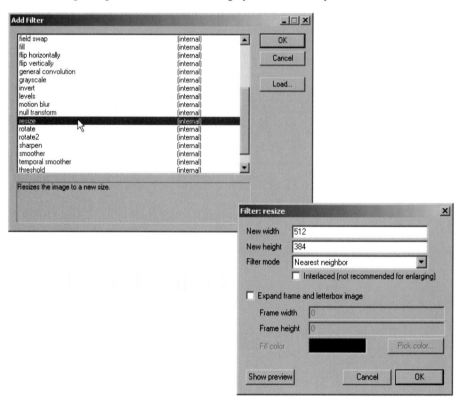

The resulting resized video is quite viewable and takes even less space on the hard drive.

Video capturing hardware – What makes sense?

The most wide-spread solution at this time is to buy a special **video capture card** with a built-in MJPEG decoder chip. This takes a big load off your processor, so you can work even with older computer hardware.

The **WinTV-PVR** card from Hauppauge allows you to record analog TV signal directly in MPEG2 format. This is a compressed format, in which data is saved on DVDs.

Satellite reception cards – **DVB-s** cards (where DVB stands for Digital Video Broadcasting) – are hot right now. This hardware, which has a promising future, receives the digital data stream from a satellite directly in MPEG2 format.

You can edit video material recorded with an MJPEG capture card in a similar manner to the one described for the Huffyuv codec.

Should you already be a proud owner of one of the two hardware components just named, your job of converting to DivX is somewhat more complex.

In the following step-by-step instructions, you learn how to get your MPEG2 video material into VirtualDub for transcoding to DivX.

Compressing the MPEG video material

Additional software for encoding MPEG2 files

You need the two programs DVD2AVI and VFAPIConv, which you can find with many other useful utilities at http://www.divx.com. The programs come without an installation routine, that is, you only have to execute them.

1 Make sure that the data stream for your MPEG2-PVR card or DVB card is saved in the *.mpg format. The accompanying software is set to save in *.pva format by default. This format cannot be edited with the common programs, however.

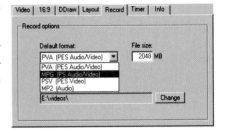

3. Visual material of near-DVD quality – The fine-tuning

Better cuts in *.pva format

The *.pva format is quite wide-spread for VCR and DVB cards and has its advantages. With the help of certain freeware tools (for example, PVACut), the video file can be cut to the targeted length even before compression. This minimizes the size of the source file (for instance, by leaving out ads), which saves computing time during compression.

2 Start recording with your usual software. Afterwards, you can view the material in *File* mode in any software DVD player. The quality of the material usually exceeds all expectations.

3 Open DVD2AVI and go to *File Open*. An Explorer window pops open. In it, select the file extension *all files* and your mpeg2 file out of the recording directory. Click *OK* to confirm your selection.

4 Your material now appears in the DVD2AVI window. Go to *File/Save Project* to create a project file that can be edited with VFAPIConv at a later time. During the conversion, you see the status display above.

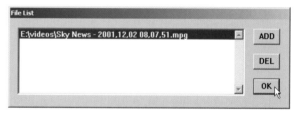

5 Now you should have two new files in your working directory: a video file with the extension *.d2v and an extracted audio stream. The latter must be attached to the video.

6 Start the program VFAPIConv and enter your two d2v files after clicking *Add Job*. Leave the settings that follow as they are and confirm them with *OK*. Afterwards, you only have to click *Convert*.

7 A quick glance at the file browser shows you the new virtual *.avi file with the extension d2v-vfapi. This file is small and is only a reference to the original video material. Its big advantage, though, is being recognized by VirtualDub. Put it to the test.

8 Open the vfapi file in VirtualDub. You can start the DivX encoding as usual.

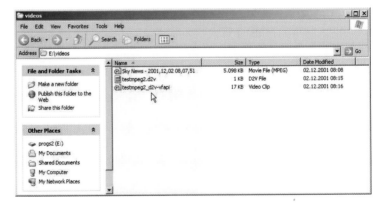

The only thing missing is the sound.

3. Visual material of near-DVD quality – The fine-tuning

Adding sound in post-production

The sound must first be converted to *.wav format. For this, you can use the DiskWriter plug-in for the popular freeware player WinAmp or any other *.wav file editor. Afterwards, the audio file is inserted, that is, the image and sound information are joined together.

9 Open the encoded video file in VirtualDub. From the *Video* menu, select *Direct stream copy*. From the *Audio* menu, select *WAV-Audio* and the *.wav file belonging to the video, as shown in the following illustration. Remember the delay value from the filename.

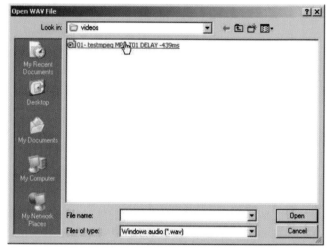

10 **Very important**: in the *Audio* menu, go to *Interleaving* and enter the delay value of the *.wav file under *Delay audio track by*. Make sure you enter the correct sign in front of the value (plus or minus)!

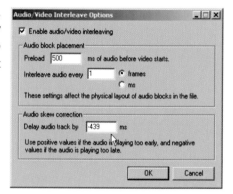

11 Even more important: in the *Video* menu, open the *Frame Rate* menu and select *Change so video and audio durations match*. VirtualDub then automatically calculates a "slant" frame rate.

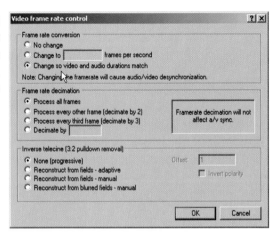

This procedure ensures image-sound synchronization. Select mp3 as the compression format again and save the avi file to be created.

Using a video recorder is admittedly easier. But when you compare the quality of the material you have just created with that of a videotape, you'll see that it was all worth the effort.

Double pass with the computer - The art of the variable bitrate

In this chapter, you discover how to create highest-end DivX material. The magic words are "two-pass encoding".

Increasing quality through variable bitrate

Variable bitrates are used to take into account motion in videos. A higher or lower bitrate is used according to whether a scene is played faster or slower, to accommodate the larger or smaller quantity of data to be processed.

For example, because of the dynamic plot, more image information has to be stored for an action scene than for the recording of a tranquil landscape. The higher the selected bitrate, the more information is saved, but also the larger the *.avi file.

3. Visual material of near-DVD quality – The fine-tuning

Two-pass encoding

In the first pass, the motion of the source material is analyzed, and the results are logged. The material is then encoded in the second pass, whereby the logged results are taken into account, and the bitrate is adapted to the film rate.

An essential advantage of two-pass encoding is the accurate calculation of the size of the *.avi file. With the help of a bitrate calculator, you can find out the exact final size of the file. This is especially important when you want to fit the final DivX video on one CD (you learn more about this in the chapter *Reserving space for the essential*).

An example of two-pass encoding

In the following steps, you encode video material in a two-pass procedure. The steps are identical in Vidomi and VirtualDub. In the following example, you encode an uncompressed *.avi file (720x480 primary resolution) in two passes in VirtualDub.

1 *Open the source material in VirtualDub. In the Audio* menu, enable the option *Direct stream copy.* Open the *Video* menu and ensure that the *Full processing mode* option is enabled. Select the codec once again by going to the *Compression* menu. Select DivX; then click *Configure* to open the *Codec Configuration* window.

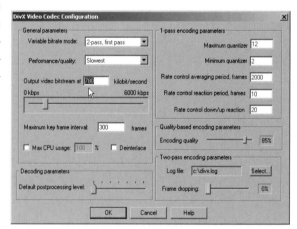

2 Select *2-pass, first pass* under *Variable bitrate mode*. Leave the default bitrate value of 780. You can experiment with it later. It is now important to select a target directory for the log file. To do so, click *Select*. The log file is then analyzed in the second pass.

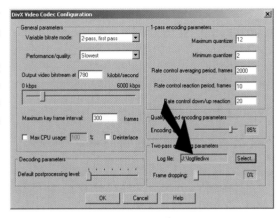

3 Now, select all the filters you deem necessary. You should at least select the *Deinterlace* filter.

4 Save the settings made so far by clicking *Save processing settings*; you might want to use the name *first_pass*. Afterwards, save the pseudo avi file obtained in the first pass under the name *videopass1*. This starts the analysis of the video.

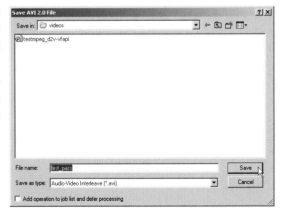

3. Visual material of near-DVD quality – The fine-tuning

5 Don't be surprised to find that the analysis takes as much time as the subsequent encoding. After the first pass, you have two new files in your video directory: a log file and a small *.avi file with the name given in the previous step. Take a look at the log file in WordPad. Note that every image was analyzed according to such criteria as complexity, motion, and texture.

```
logdivx - WordPad                                                      _|□|x|
File  Edit  View  Insert  Format  Help

 D|☞|🖫| 🖨|🔍| 🏿| 🖫| 🖫| 🖫| ~| 🖫|

##version 2
quality 3
Frame 0: intra 1, quant 4, texture 382142, motion 0, total 382142, complexity 4776775
Frame 1: intra 0, quant 4, texture 186747, motion 9166, total 213393, complexity 2334337
Frame 2: intra 0, quant 5, texture 135917, motion 7593, total 157964, complexity 2718339
Frame 3: intra 0, quant 5, texture 141206, motion 8961, total 165896, complexity 2824119
Frame 4: intra 0, quant 6, texture 114185, motion 8044, total 138299, complexity 3568281
Frame 5: intra 0, quant 6, texture 103648, motion 6932, total 121813, complexity 3238999
Frame 6: intra 0, quant 7, texture 102917, motion 9079, total 127314, complexity 4678045
Frame 7: intra 0, quant 7, texture 93280, motion 8787, total 116954, complexity 4240000
Frame 8: intra 0, quant 7, texture 108414, motion 8909, total 131681, complexity 4927909
Frame 9: intra 0, quant 7, texture 89083, motion 7827, total 113833, complexity 4049227
Frame 10: intra 0, quant 7, texture 95270, motion 8149, total 117569, complexity 4330454
Frame 11: intra 0, quant 7, texture 82681, motion 7722, total 105364, complexity 3758227
Frame 12: intra 0, quant 7, texture 100034, motion 8117, total 123958, complexity 4547000
Frame 13: intra 0, quant 7, texture 91742, motion 8174, total 113288, complexity 4170090
Frame 14: intra 0, quant 7, texture 99176, motion 7538, total 120426, complexity 4508000
Frame 15: intra 0, quant 7, texture 78203, motion 7542, total 98686, complexity 3554681
Frame 16: intra 0, quant 7, texture 88446, motion 6682, total 108289, complexity 4020272
Frame 17: intra 0, quant 7, texture 84946, motion 7614, total 107003, complexity 3861181
Frame 18: intra 0, quant 8, texture 76033, motion 6391, total 93769, complexity 4472529
Frame 19: intra 0, quant 8, texture 65250, motion 7229, total 85601, complexity 3838235
Frame 20: intra 0, quant 8, texture 79487, motion 6099, total 98406, complexity 4675705
Frame 21: intra 0, quant 8, texture 76641, motion 7074, total 96729, complexity 4508293
Frame 22: intra 0, quant 8, texture 88898, motion 7717, total 110048, complexity 5229293
Frame 23: intra 0, quant 8, texture 78503, motion 6764, total 98277, complexity 4617823
Frame 24: intra 0, quant 8, texture 87721, motion 6667, total 108552, complexity 5160058

For Help, press F1                                                       |NUM|
```

6 For the second pass, select the option *2-pass, second pass*, and ensure that the correct log file has been chosen. Then, save the final file as *filmpass2.avi*, which starts the actual encoding. Afterwards, you can admire the completed video on your player.

You should notice a definite improvement in quality, especially for dynamic scenes. For such scenes, one-pass encoded material tends to form blocks.

Saving time by shortening the first pass

You can save time for the entire encoding process by canceling the first pass after a few minutes. VirtualDub still creates a log file for the frames played, which are usually representative for the whole film.

DivX decoded – The parameters

If you haven't already done so, you might feel the urge to experiment with the codec on your own now.

But what do all the cryptic parameters in the *Codec Configuration window* mean? The following table enlightens you.

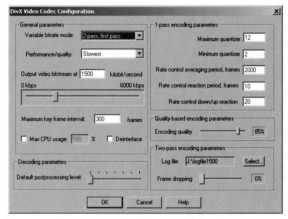

Parameter	Meaning
Variable bitrate mode	Choose between one-pass and two-pass encoding.
Performance/quality	The faster the encoding, the lower the quality of the material is. The "Fastest" mode is best suited to on-the-fly capturing.
Output video bitstream	Manually choose the bitrate used during encoding. The bitrate is set for one-pass encoding.
Maximum key frame interval	The maximum interval between two key frames. You can only cut between key frames. See below for more information.
Max. CPU usage	Should not be set to 100% if possible (except if you are letting the computer run overnight).
Default postprocessing level	There are 6 levels of post-processing in the interest of optimizing the picture quality; level 6 (maximal quality) is located to the far right.
Maximum/Minimum quantizer	For the constant bitrate mode. Rule of thumb: the lower the quantizer, the better the quality but also the larger the amount of data.
Rate control options	Influences the reaction time in the variable bitrate mode; should not be changed if possible.

3. Visual material of near-DVD quality – The fine-tuning

Parameter	Meaning
Encoding quality	Self-explanatory; the better the encoding quality, the slower the encoding process.
Log file	This shows the target directory for the log file in the two-pass process.
Frame dropping	Establishes whether frame dropping is allowed. This can some-times lead to jumps during playback.

Note

Compression formats and key frames

The concept of key frames always comes up when talking of video compression. The trick with most compression algorithms is to select certain frames as reference or key frames and to save the deviations from the key frame for all the following frames.

Consider a train passing through a landscape. The "empty" landscape is saved as a key frame, while the following frames only contain deviations to the landscape caused by the passing train.

The disadvantage of this method is that compressed material can only be cut from key frame to key frame.

Note

VirtualDub and its options

Because you are using only a few of the filters in VirtualDub (which are explained for this purpose), those who desire a more detailed description of the program should consider the following book:

Fast Bytes/Creating Video CDs by Mark-Steffen Göwecke, published by DATA BECKER.

4. Timed recordings

You are missing just one more feature for turning your computer into a full-scale video recorder: the option of programming the time for your recording. A number of different programs with such imposing sounding names as "PowerVCR" are already out on the market. The disadvantage of such a complete solution is that the DivX support is usually missing.

> **Note**
>
> **All-in-one solutions: PowerVCR II and WinVCR**
>
> The following are two addresses where you can download such programs, should you be interested in testing a commercial PC-VCR solution. For a trial version of PowerVCR II, go to:
>
> http://www.cyberlink.com.tw/english/products/powervcr2/powervcr2.asp
>
> You can obtain WinVCR at:
>
> http://www.cinax.com/Products/winvcr.html

The best solution, however, is to add a timer feature to VirtualDub. You can do this with the help of *Windows Scripting Host* and *Windows Scheduled Tasks*:

- **Windows Scripting Host (WSH)** facilitates the automation of key combinations for Windows programs and is the equivalent of the good old batch file under DOS. WHS is a regular component of the operating system since Windows 98.

- **Windows Scheduled Tasks** ensures that programs are started or ended on a certain schedule.

To add a timer feature to VirtualDub, follow this procedure:

Automating VirtualDub

1 Open a Windows text editor of your choice (such as WordPad) and enter the following script code (each apostrophe is followed by a commentary):

```
'VBS script for starting VirtualDub in immediate capture mode
set WSHShell = wscript.CreateObject("Wscript.Shell")
'Define shell object
```

```
WSHShell.run "d:\virtualdub\virtualdub.exe"
'Start VirtualDub (please enter the correct path)
wscript.sleep 2000
'Wait 2 seconds (so the program can start)
WSHShell.Sendkeys "%f{p}"
'Enable the VirtualDub capture mode with ALT+f+p
'wscript.sleep 1000 'Wait 1 second
WSHShell.Sendkeys "{F6}" 'Start the recording with F6
```

This means that the script starts VirtualDub, goes into *Capture* mode, and starts a recording.

2 Save the script as a text document under the following name: *startvdub.vbs*. Windows later recognizes this file as Visual Basic Script. Acknowledge the warning illustrated below with *Yes*.

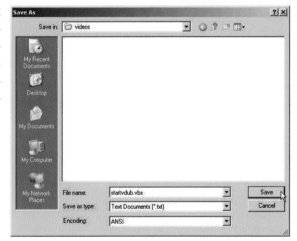

3 The script now appears in the directory of your choice with the typical Visual Basic Script icon. To test the script, double-click it to execute it. This should launch VirtualDub, and the capturing should start after a short pause.

startvdub

Using Windows Scheduled Tasks

The system now needs to be programmed to start the script created above at a given time. For this, use Windows Scheduled Tasks, which is a regular component of every modern Microsoft Windows operating system.

1 In the Start menu, go to *All Programs/ Accessories/System Tools*. Click *Scheduled Tasks* to start the task manager.

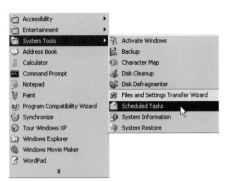

2 Click *Add Scheduled Task*. This launches a Wizard that takes you through the following menus. Acknowledge the Wizard's greeting by clicking *Next*.

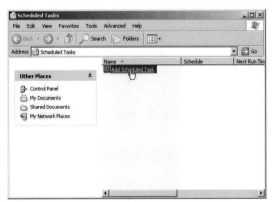

3 A window opens, in which you can select the program you want to schedule. The programs displayed here are only those known to the system. To select the script you just created, click *Browse* and search for your VirtualDub start script in the Explorer window. Click the filename and then *Open*.

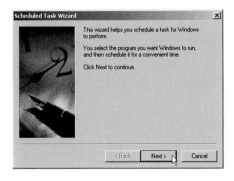
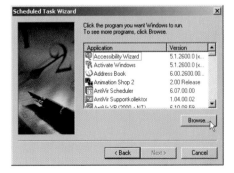

4. Timed recordings

4 Here you can give the task a new name (for example, that of the program you want to record, to maintain an overview). Select to perform the task one time only (unless you want to record a program that airs daily, and so forth.). Then move on to the next window.

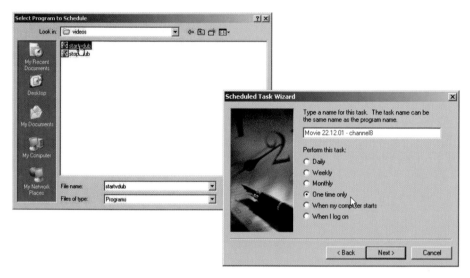

4 In the current window, enter the start time and date for the show. Confirm your selection with *Next*. If you don't own a Windows 2000 or Windows XP system, skip the next step, in which you need to enter the username and password of the user assigned to the task.

5 This is it. You can now leave the Wizard by clicking *Finish*. The task you just scheduled appears in the *Scheduled Tasks* system folder.

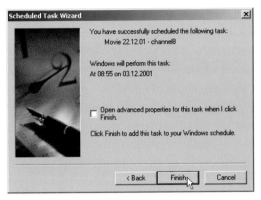

Our PC video recorder has only one defect: once VirtualDub is started, it mercilessly fills your hard drive, for you haven't yet set any conditions for stopping it. You can stop the recording in one of two ways.

Controlled canceling of the recording

* 1st alternative:

Use the integrated stop function of VirtualDub. In *Capture* mode, open the *Stop conditions* window from the *Open* menu and set the length of the video you want to record. You need to use your math, for the length must be given in seconds. The neighboring window shows how to record an hour of video material, for instance. Then, you must save the settings you just adjusted by going to *Preferences/Save current capture settings*.

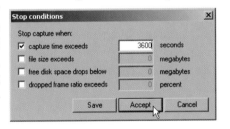

* 2nd alternative:

Write a VBS script analogous to the start script, accept this time for stopping VirtualDub, and then enter it in the *Scheduled Tasks* folder using the task manager as described above. The stop script could look as follows:

```
'VBS script for stopping VirtualDub in immediate capture mode
set WSHShell = wscript.CreateObject("Wscript.Shell")
'Define shell object
WSHShell.SendKeys "ESC"
```

4. Timed recordings

```
'End recording with ESC
WSHShell.SendKeys "%f{x}"
'Exit capture mode
WSHShell.SendKeys "%f{q}"
'Close VirtualDub cleanly
```

This allows you to end the recording at a predetermined time. Please consider, however, that TV stations don't always keep to their own published schedules, and that we don't yet have VPS for the computer.

A convenient front end is also possible

Note

If you search for *VirtualDub as video recorder* with any search engine (don't put the search term within quotation marks, however), sooner or later you find front ends for Windows Scripting Host, which realizes the feature presented above with a nice interface. You might want to check www.virtualdub.org to see if any front ends are available for VirtualDub.

5. The Internet, the global video store

This chapter discloses the possibilities of **legally** sharing in the largest video store in the world – and I say *sharing* because you can call up as well as supply DivX videos. The mysterious abbreviation *p2p* (which stands for *peer-to-peer*) plays an important role in it.

A peer-to-peer network is a two-way connection in the Internet, connecting logged-on computers with each other with the help of p2p clients. Such a peer-to-peer connection allows for the easy transfer of data from one computer to another. The advantage is that you don't need a central computer for organizing or cataloging the offered data collection.

The content of the files you offer or acquire by p2p is, of course, subject to copyright law. For this reason, please note the following warning:

Only trade videos that you created yourself or that were officially released for this purpose!

The publisher, DATA BECKER, and the author expressly distance themselves from the trade of illegal DivX video content. Please be aware that the trade of illegally created or acquired DivX videos can have serious legal consequences.

The simplest solution for configuring your computer as a p2p client is called *Morpheus*, the peer-to-peer client from Musiccity. You can download the program from http://www.musiccity.com.

Configuring Morpheus and registering with the p2p network

So, you have downloaded Morpheus from the address above, and now you want to install the program and register as a user in the Morpheus net. To do this, proceed as follows:

5. The Internet, the global video store

1 Double-click the icon of the downloaded Morpheus installation program. Confirm the licensing agreement and select the installation directory.

2 The program is then installed. At the end, enable the option *Do not start Morpheus automatically at startup,* for this is only useful for those who connect over a dedicated line. Close the setup by clicking *Finish*.

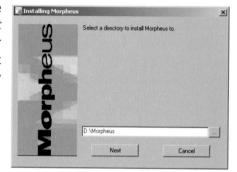

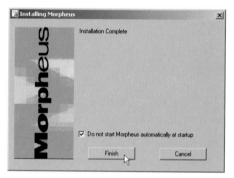

3 The program then tries to connect to the Internet and the Musiccity server. Once the connection is set up, a Wizard helps you create a user account. Acknowledge the Wizard's greeting window.

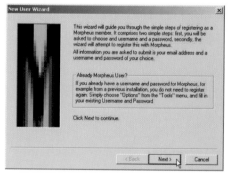

4 In the next window, enter your desired username, select a password and confirm it. Finally, also enter your e-mail address. Write down your registration data and continue by clicking *Next*. A status bar appears that shows you the progress of your registration.

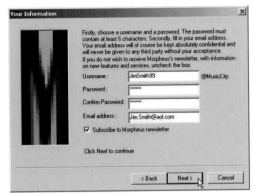

Staying anonymous with Morpheus – Enter a screen name

A screen name is a pseudonym. When registering with Morpheus, you can enter a made-up name and e-mail address, for the Morpheus server doesn't (yet) do a background check.

---

5 If you can see this window, you are registered with the Morpheus network.

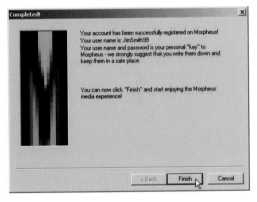

Now you can go hunt for DivX to your heart's content. Simply go online and start the Morpheus program.

Online with Morpheus

The following start screen accompanies you as of now when doing your research with Morpheus:

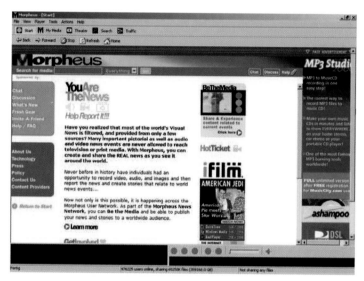

As you can see, it is a perfectly normal browser front end with just one little but important difference in the upper-left corner of the window, where you can find additional buttons for navigating the central information system. They have the following meaning:

Button	Function
Start	Back to the start page
My Media	File view of your downloaded files
Theater	Built-in preview mode
Search	Here you can start the search by media
Traffic	View of the current data traffic and transfer of selected files

Perform a search with Morpheus. An entirely legitimate search would be the hunt for a current movie trailer in DivX format, for these are officially placed onto the

Internet by movie companies for the purpose of advertising and are available for downloading.

1 Start Morpheus and click *Search* on the upper menu bar. (*Hint*: Because the Morpheus server is sometimes overloaded, you might need some patience until the button is not shaded anymore). The following search window appears. Select the *Video* option.

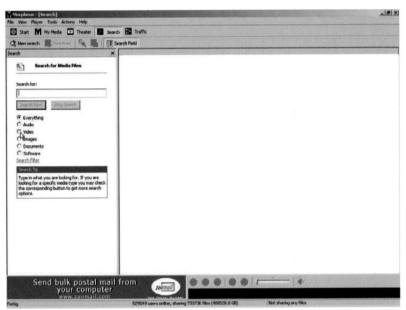

2 The search window changes to limit the search to video material. Enter the name of the desired trailer and add *divx* to the end of the query. Start the search by clicking *Search Now*.

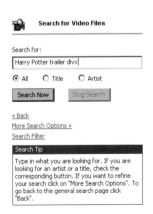

5. The Internet, the global video store

3 After a little while, the program displays your search results. In front of some results, you see a plus sign, as you know it from the file view in Windows Explorer. Click the plus sign to view all the files belonging to the main entry, which are saved in other places on the Internet in identical form.

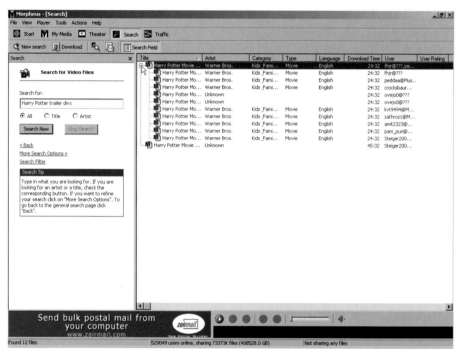

78

4 Close the directory tree view of the file by clicking the plus sign and select the desired file or group of files. Double-click or click the menu item *Download* to start downloading. Now switch to the *Traffic* window. There, you should see the selected file. The download should start automatically after a little while. Click the plus sign to view all the places involved in transferring the file.

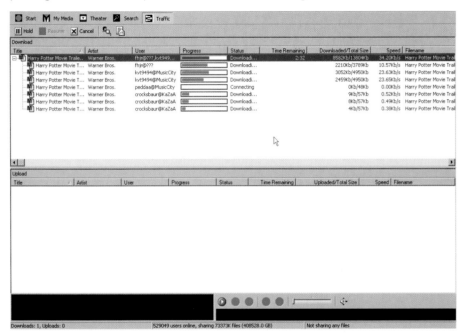

5 While downloading, you already have the possibility of viewing the material. Right-click the file being transferred to open a pop-up menu. Select *Preview/Play* to start playing back the video in the *Theater*, which you can reach by clicking the corresponding button. (*Hint*: Because the Morpheus software is still being developed, this doesn't always function.)

5. The Internet, the global video store

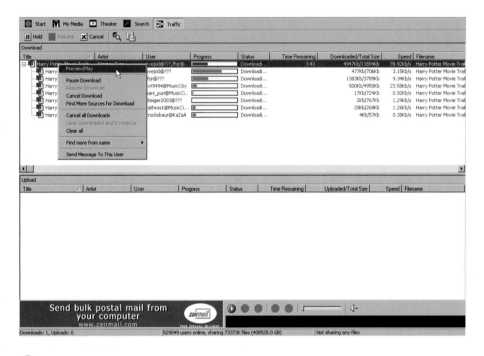

6 Once the download is complete, you can peacefully view your file in the *Theater*.

The DivX bazaar: Trading videos

Thanks to the constantly increasing bandwidths and optimized data compression processes like DivX, the Internet is becoming the place where video material is traded. The contents you can find on the Web are multiplying exponentially. One reason is that more and more people are sharing in peer-to-peer exchanges.

But how can you contribute your own contents, such as an excerpt from your last vacation video, for instance, meant to give interested travelers a first impression of the destination? Note the following steps.

1 Start Windows Explorer and copy the files you want to exchange to *My Shared Folder* of the Morpheus installation directory.

2 Next, start Morpheus and open the internal file browser by clicking *My Media*. This opens a directory structure similar to that of Windows Explorer, which displays all the files you have downloaded. Your newly added file(s) appear in the *Unknown* directory of the corresponding file type (here, under the *"Video"* category.

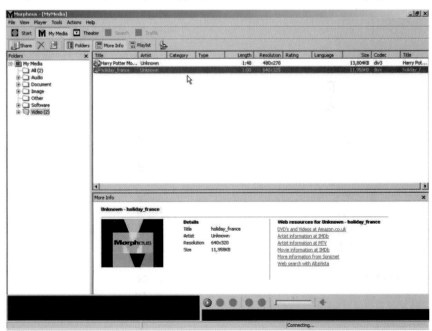

5. The Internet, the global video store

3 It is now important to catalog your video for those searching on the Internet. Right-click the file you want to catalog and select *Edit Details*. The pop-up menu opens, in which you should first assign the video to different categories.

4 The menu *More* is particularly important. Here, you can enter the keywords that are transmitted to the search engine for searches with Morpheus. A short description of the file content also helps the searchers. After entering all information, confirm by clicking *OK*.

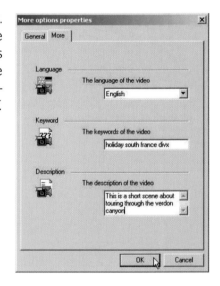

Finally, you discover that Morpheus has assigned your file to the "correct" category. Nothing stands in the way of an exchange on the Internet now.

Exploiting Morpheus to its full capacity – The options

Under *Tools/Options*, you can open dialog windows for different configurations, which are explained in the following:

The User option

In this window, you can find your user data. This is especially useful if you have installed Morpheus on a new computer and don't want to re-register the program. In addition, Morpheus can automatically notify you of any program updates that have been released.

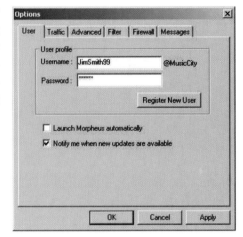

The Traffic option

This option displays the directory in which the files you are offering for trade are saved. You can limit the number of simultaneous downloads for the optimal use of the bandwidth at your disposal. You can also limit the number of uploads, which prevents a situation in which too many users are downloading files from your computer simultaneously, thus occupying your bandwidth. If you can avoid it, don't check the option *Disable sharing of files*. This

83

prevents other users from downloading from your computer, which goes against Morpheus netiquette.

The Advanced option

Here, you can limit the number of re-sults displayed for each search. You can also limit the bandwidth for uploading or disable the option of functioning as a SuperNode. A SuperNode is an interme-diary between several Morpheus clients. Avoid becoming a SuperNode, if pos-sible, to save bandwidth for your own downloads.

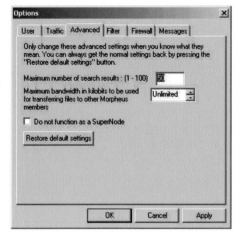

The Filter option

In the *Filter* menu, you can explicitly ex-clude files containing certain keywords or contents that potentially contain vi-ruses. The first mark blocks files that potentially contain viruses (for example, Windows Scripts). If you have a firewall, also select the second filter. The third filter blocks the downloading of illegal video and music files.

Filters keep your PC clean

If you have enabled all filters, you can be pretty sure that you are legally safe as far as the material downloaded is concerned. In addition, you can obtain minimal protection against viruses, which doesn't release you, of course, from running an active **virus scanner** in the background.

The Firewall option only concerns special cases. The Messages option is another.

The Messages option

Sometimes it might be important to keep certain people from contacting you directly through Morpheus. Add such unpleasant individuals to the *Ignore List*. You can also block all queries by enabling the option *Ignore all incoming messages*.

6. Movies without commercials and channel logos

If you don't want to put up with commercial interruptions, the next tutorial is for you. Here, you learn how you can free source material from pesky commercial breaks with VirtualDub. In addition, you can also tackle another pest: those annoying channel logos.

Sharp cuts with VirtualDub

Removing commercial blocks makes sense from two points of view: for one, it avoids the interruptions of the movie flow mentioned above; for the other, it reduces the encoding time, which depends on the amount of data contained by the source material, as you know. The following describes how to cut video material with VirtualDub. The material to be cut can be compressed or uncompressed.

> **Taking the beginning and final credits into consideration when recording**
>
> As with the good old video recorder, you should program the time for the movie you want to record generously (that is, you should allow about 5 minutes of beginning and final credits). Cutting the material afterwards is easy.

1 Start VirtualDub and go into *File* mode. Load the file you want to edit. Use the slider to scroll through the movie and search for the approximate beginning of the commercial block. Scroll to a spot immediately preceding the commercial break.

2 Use the *key* arrows to carefully advance to the exact spot where the movie segment ends (this is a move towards the next key frame). A fade-out is usually interposed here, so the last frame is black.

3 Select the beginning of the commercial block by clicking *Mark in*. The time offset of the current frame then appears at the bottom of the window.

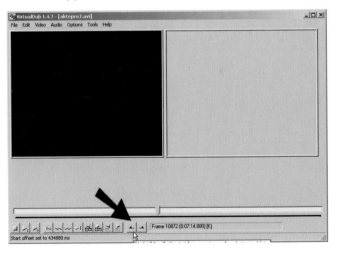

6. Movies without commercials and channel logos

4 Now search for the end of the commercial block as described in step 2. Select the end by clicking *Mark out*. The *End offset* value appears on the bottom left of the window, and the segment to be cut is highlighted in blue on the movie timeline.

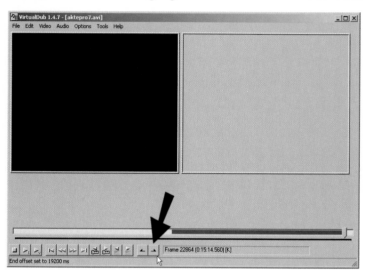

5 Select the *Delete frames* command from the *Edit* menu (or press (Del)). The commercial block is then deleted.

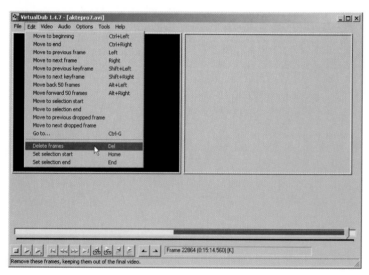

6 Repeat steps 2 through 5 until your movie is commercial-free.

Moving from scene to scene with the Scene buttons

If you want to roughly search for scene changes, use the *Scene* buttons, which are pointed out by an arrow in the following illustration.

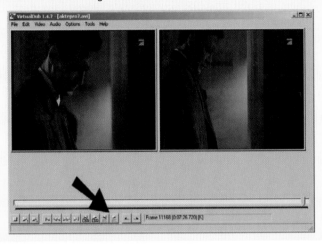

7 When saving, make sure that both the video and audio editor options *Direct stream copy* are selected, for you are not encoding yet. Save the cut material under a new name by going to *File/Save as AVI* (or by pressing F7).

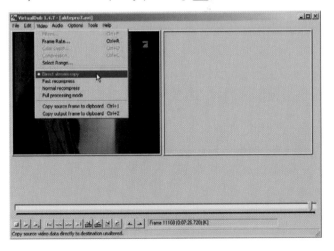

6. Movies without commercials and channel logos

First cut, then encode

Save valuable computation time by freeing the video material from commercial blocks before encoding it. You can thus save several hours of encoding time when you do a two-pass encoding!

Owners of DVBs and MPEG2 hardware should take the following tip seriously.

Pre-cut PVA recordings with PVACut

Digital satellite streams or PVR files can be roughly cut with PVACut before being edited with VirtualDub. This is important for preserving the synchronization between the audio and video streams. If you are working only with VirtualDub, you must insert the audio stream before cutting and cut it with the video stream; otherwise, major synchronization problems result.

Fast cutting: The most important keyboard shortcuts

For cutting purposes, it is often more convenient to use a few effective keyboard shortcuts to navigate through the movie. You can reach the cutting functions over the *Edit* menu.

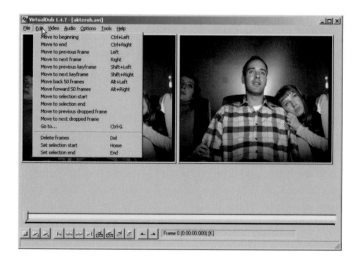

The following table gives you an overview of the most important shortcuts in the *Edit* menu.

Keyboard shortcut	Effect
Ctrl + Left	Goes to the beginning of the movie.
Ctrl + Right	Goes to the end of the movie.
Left	Goes one frame back.
Right	Goes one frame foreward.
Shift + Left	Goes to the previous key frame.
Shift + Right	Goes to the next key frame.
Alt + Left	Goes back 50 frames.
Alt + Right	Goes foreward 50 frames.
Home	Defines the beginning of a selection.
End	Defines the end of a selection.
Ctrl + G	Goes to a certain frame or time marker.

Note

About frames and key frames

The compression codec creates *key frames* at regular intervals, which are used to compute the following images. Only the deviations from the key frame are then saved as data material, which saves hard drive space.

A *frame* is an individual image in a video stream.

Important: With VirtualDub, you can only cut from one key frame to the next, but this smart program keeps that in mind by itself.

Getting rid of logos with LogoAway

One of the outstanding characteristics of VirtualDub is the ease with which it can be extended. You can use plug-ins to incorporate just about any feature into the program. These plug-ins are available as filters. You have already learned about the *Deinterlace* filter, which is part of the program package, in the chapter *Visual material of near-DVD quality*.

On the VirtualDub Web site, you can find a multitude of links to third-party software, offering further interesting and free plug-ins. In the following, you install and use such a plug-in – the LogoAway filter by Krystof Wojdon.

6. Movies without commercials and channel logos

Installing LogoAway

You can officially download LogoAway at

http://www.republika.pl/vander74/virtualdub/

After downloading the program, proceed as follows:

1 Unpack the zip archive. It contains only a small file named *logoaway.vdf*.

2 Copy the file to the *Plugins* folder in your VirtualDub working directory.

logoaway.vdf

3 Start VirtualDub and go to *Video/ Filters/Add*. LogoAway now appears as a new filter.

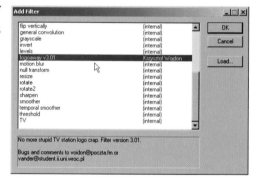

Note

When installing plug-ins, only copy them to the directory!
You can install all VirtualDub extensions in this way. You can even design your own filters with the help of a filter kit (available on the VirtualDub home page).

Using LogoAway

Load a video bearing a logo into VirtualDub. You can now remove the logo effortlessly.

1 First, select a frame in which the logo you want to remove is as clearly visible as possible. A dark background is best for this.

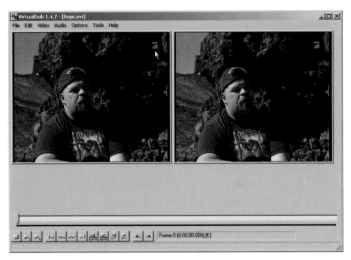

2 Now, select the filter by going to *Video/Filters/Add.../logoaway*. The Logo Away configuration window opens. Check the *Visible borders* option and click *Show preview*.

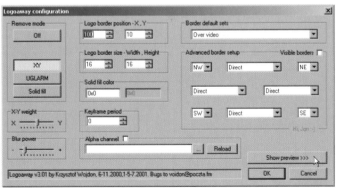

3 A small dotted square now appears in the upper-left corner of the preview window. You can adapt it to the position and size of the logo with the help of the *Logo border* spin boxes.

6. Movies without commercials and channel logos

4 Move the dotted frame over the channel logo with the help of the *Logo border position* and *Logo border size* spin boxes, until the logo is framed in its entirety. The logo disappears. **Important**: After positioning the LogoAway frame, disable the *Visible borders* option; otherwise, the frame is encoded with the image. Confirm your settings with *OK*.

5 The settings you just made are shown in the *Filters* window. Here, you can also crop the frame by clicking *Cropping*, because most TV programs are broadcast with black bars. You learn more about this in the chapter *Reserving space for the essential*, however.

6 Quit the *Filters* window by clicking *OK*. For further editing, set VirtualDub to *Full processing mode*; otherwise, the filter doesn't take effect.

> **Filtering and encoding in one go**
>
> You should filter and encode the video material all at once, because the video material has to be cached into a temporary file while you are using a filter, which takes up space.

Now, adjust the encoding settings as described in the fine-tuning chapter, *Save as AVI*, and your video is now completely without commercials.

Note

The filtering modes of LogoAway

Until now, the author of LogoAway has implemented three different filtering modes:

- **XY**: Here, the logo is wiped out horizontally and vertically.
- **UGLARM**: A more complex, more effective (but also slower) algorithm by a third party.

  Solid fill: Here, you paint over the logo with a predefined color.
- Finally, there is also **Off**, which means that there is no filter effect. You can use this mode for control.

Filters: It's all about the correct sequence

By the time you have worked through the last section, you have discovered that using several filters during encoding can be tricky.

Let's assume you have captured a video in full resolution and are now planning both to change the resolution and to treat the video with the LogoAway filter. In addition, you also want to remove the pesky artifacts by deinterlacing. Therefore, you have to use filters. Choose the following sequence:

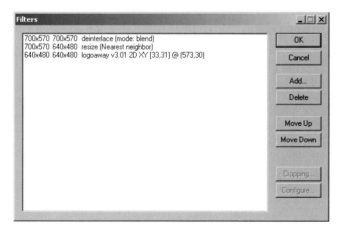

Here's an explanation:

- You should first apply the deinterlace filter to the video material in full resolution. At this point, you might want to crop the black bars around the images. (You should do this before you resize at any rate; otherwise, you obtain artifacts.)

- Afterwards, change the resolution of the images both in the x and the y directions in **multiples of 16**.

- Only now should you employ the LogoAway filter. This way, you ensure that the filter algorithm changes as few pixels as possible.

The result is worth watching.

Applying the finishing touches to the logo: Precision retouching with the alpha channel

The XY-blurring technique (meaning the blurring of image information in a rectangular region) used for retouching until now has the disadvantage that few commercial logos are exactly rectangular. It would be nice if you had a blurring mask that fit precisely to the shape of the logo.

LogoAway's author has also implemented this option, called the alpha channel masking technique. The following tutorial shows you how this is implemented. In addition to VirtualDub, you merely require a pixel-oriented image-editing program such as Paint Shop Pro, for example.

96

1 Define a rectangular masking region with LogoAway, as described above. The area should be selected relatively generously, and it should be relatively square (for example, 30x30 pixels). Select *Visible borders*.

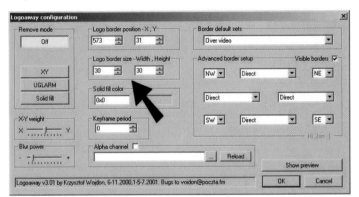

2 Within the LogoAway plugin, go to *Preview*. Select a frame that distinguishes the logo well from the background (for example, a light logo on a dark background).

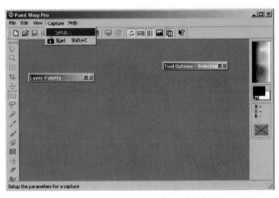

3 Open the image-editing program of your choice. Look for a menu for taking screenshots (the *File/Import/Screen Capture* menu in Paint Shop Pro). Go

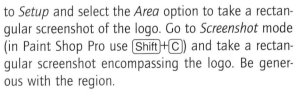

to *Setup* and select the *Area* option to take a rectangular screenshot of the logo. Go to *Screenshot* mode (in Paint Shop Pro use (Shift)+(C)) and take a rectangular screenshot encompassing the logo. Be generous with the region.

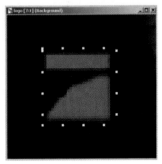

6. Movies without commercials and channel logos

4 Zoom into the logo so that the pixels are clearly visible. Select the square region around the logo, including the border pixels, with a rectangular selection tool. Copy the selection to a new image (in Paint Shop Pro, use Ctrl+C and then Ctrl+V).

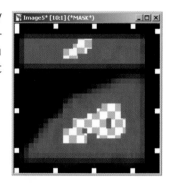

5 Now select a masking tool (in Paint Shop Pro, go to *Masks/New/Show all*, followed by *Masks/Edit*). Select the pencil tool and delete all the logo's pixels individually (but **not** the ones marking the border!). The background appears, usually a gray/black checkered area.

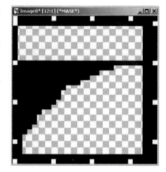

6 Go to *Edit/Copy* and *Edit/Paste As New Image* to transfer the mask as a new image. The transparent regions are replaced by the respective current foreground color. To ultimately use the image with VirtualDub, it has to be inverted by going to *Colors/Negative Image*. Finally, save the finished image as a *.bmp file (Bitmap).

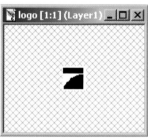

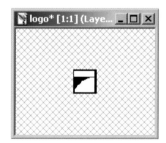

Note

Adjusting the size of the bitmap for VirtualDub

Verify that the image size meets VirtualDub's requirements by going to *View Image Information* (above: 30x30 pixels). Otherwise, scale the image to the correct size by going to *Resize*. And please use the *.bmp format exclusively for saving, because compressed formats such as *.jpg are not (yet) supported by the plug-in.

7 Now, back to VirtualDub: Check *Alpha Channel* and select your bitmap mask from the *Alpha channel* menu. Have a look at the expected results in the *Preview* mode. Do not forget to remove the checkmark from *Visible borders* before starting the encoding.

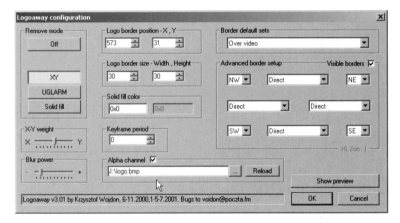

Complicated? True, but the result impresses you so much that it makes all the trouble seem worthwhile.

Self-advertising – Integrating your own logo into the movie

After you have successfully removed all the commercial traces from the movie clip, the question arises if you can also integrate your own logo into the movie afterwards.

6. Movies without commercials and channel logos

You require a further external filter for VirtualDub to integrate the logo. It is called Logo Filter, was created by Donald Graft, and can be downloaded from http://sauron.mordor.net/dgraft/. There, you can also find other exceptional filters.

The filter named *Logo.vdf* is installed into the VirtualDub plug-in directory in the way described for the LogoAway filter.

Integrating a static logo ...

The following instructions help you overlay any video clip with the transparent design of your choice.

1 Open a pixel-oriented image-editing program (for example, Paint Shop Pro). Set an RGB value of 0/0/255 by clicking the field for the background color. This is of consequence if you want to place the logo transparently in front of the clip.

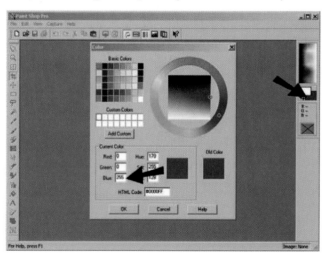

2 Create a new image. As a test, use the properties above. A window opens, in which you can use the text tool to enter some characters for a logo. Use white as the font color. In addition, the anti-aliasing function should **not** be used because this might lead to pixel artifacts in the video.

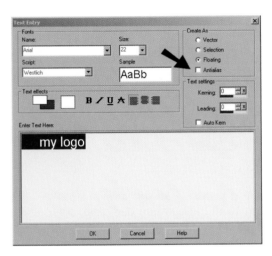

3 Save the newly created logo as a *.bmp file in the directory of your choice. If necessary, you can first use the *Crop* tool to make the logo smaller.

4 Now, load the video clip in VirtualDub and, if necessary, define some pre-filters (deinterlace, resize, LogoAway) as described above. Select the logo filter by going to the menu item *Video/Filters*. The corresponding dialog window appears. Under *Input file*, give the path of the logo you created. To use the transparency effect, select *Enable* and set the transparency color to *Blue 255*.

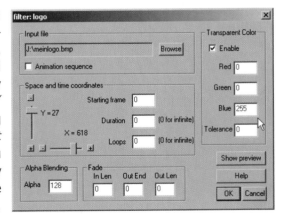

6. Movies without commercials and channel logos

5 Click *Preview* to see the preview. Use the X and Y sliders in the logo filter window to move your logo to the desired position, most preferably to the position of the original logo. Close the filter window by clicking *OK* and begin the conversion. (Don't forget to select a codec.)

... or an animation!

You are naturally not restricted to the integration of simple, static text as additional image content. On the plug-in author's home page, notice the example of how a dynamic bitmap can be integrated. The example is a rotating globe but no limits are set to your imagination for realizing your wildest creations.

1 First, download the sample *Animated rotated earth demo* from the Web site specified above and unzip it to the directory of your choice. Open the logo filter dialog window.

2 Select the first image of the bitmap sequence as the *Input file* and check the *Animation sequence* box, as well as the *Enable* box under *Transparent Color*. Set an RGB value of 0/0/0, because the background of the incorporated image is black. Leave the rest of the values in the window unchanged. These are explained at the end of the section.

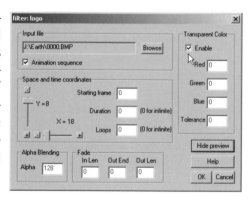

3 Again, examine the settings you have made in the *Preview* window. Afterwards, start the encoding process.

The options for the logo filter:

The following table explains the options for the logo filter for your personal experimentation.

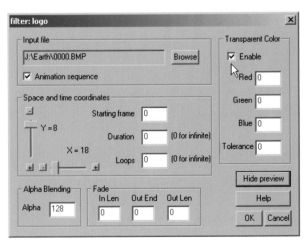

6. Movies without commercials and channel logos

Parameter	Effect
Input file	Name and location of the logo bitmap file
Animation sequence	Use an animated logo
X/Y sliders	Set the position of the logo
Starting frame	Frame in which the logo should first appear
Duration	Length of time the logo should appear ("0" = infinite)
Loops	Number of loops the logo should be displayed for
Alpha Blending	Degree to which the film should be overlayed (255 = logo completely overlays the film)
Fade options	Logo fade-in/fade-out
Transparent Color options	Use a transparent background color for the logo

7. Reserving space for the essential

This chapter explains how to fit an entire, relatively good-quality movie onto a normal CD-ROM.

> **Space restrictions due to blank CD capacity**
>
> Four different types of blank CDs are currently available:
>
> - The **650 MB** blank CD (the 74-minute blank CD)
> - The **700 MB** blank CD (the 80-minute blank CD)
> - The **800 MB** blank CD (the 90-minute blank CD)
> - The **870 MB** blank CD (the 99-minute blank CD)
>
> In comparison, a simple DVD has a capacity of 4.7 GB.

The times indicated in the box refer to audio or video material.

Because every commercially available burner does not support the 870 MB blank CD, the following instructions are restricted to the creation of DivX files with a maximum size of 700 MB, which can then be conveniently dealt with in the chapter *Transferring DivX material onto CD*. The instructions can, however, also be applied to the creation of 870 MB file sizes without any problems.

All the techniques described in this chapter apply to DVD material as well as to material captured directly from TV (Huffyuv, MJPEG or mpeg2), so that no more distinction is made between them in the following.

The first tutorial starts with a lesson in the art of exclusion.

The film exceeds the frame

One of the main frustrations with digital movie material occurs when the viewer watches the movie in a software player or even in VirtualDub.

7. Reserving space for the essential

In the above image, the black bars were highlighted with white lines for emphasis.

A large part of the image in modern movies contains only visual excess because of the black bars, unless you are viewing it on a modern 16:9 TV. This also has a noticeable negative impact when encoding.

Note

Sharp borders increase the quantity of data

Most of the video compression techniques function by saving fewer pixels as well as the information of neighboring pixels. If the transition in a part of the image is extreme – as it is with the black bars – substantially more information must then be saved, and the amount of data for the frame or the film is increased.

Well then, away with the black bars ...

Removing the bars, but properly

1 Open the movie material to be edited in VirtualDub. Correctly trimming the film necessitates the selection of at least one filter. If you haven't defined any other filter, go to *Video/Filters/Add Filter* and select the *null transform* filter. This action makes it possible for you to crop the film directly.

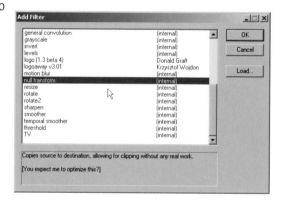

2 Confirm by clicking *OK*. In the next window, click *Cropping*.

Cropping – integrated into almost every filter

The cropping function can be found according to the filter definitions for almost all filter types.

3 In the cropping window that appears, you can use the *offset* spin boxes to trim both the height and the width of the borders. Pay attention to symmetric offsets as in the present example. (This means that the values for the X1/X2 offsets should be identical with the ones for the Y1/Y2 offsets.) Confirm the changes by clicking *OK*. Make sure to crop more than necessary to avoid any artifacts from leftover borders (see the info box further up).

7. Reserving space for the essential

Format is a matter of taste – Experiment!

You can crop the film to your own format; for instance, if you want to display a movie in 4:3 format on the television. This can be accomplished by cutting off the right and left edges of the film.

4 The changed values for the image dimensions appear in the filter dialog window. If necessary, note the values and acknowledge them by clicking *OK*.

5 Now let the finished cropped image amaze you in VirtualDub's *Preview* window.

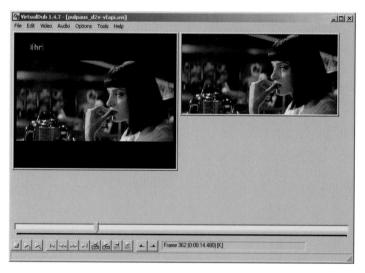

You cannot start encoding until you have considered the following problem:

Always select image dimensions in multiples of 16!

Few graphics cards are currently available on the market that can correctly display DivX image formats, whose height and width are not multiples of 16. The blame goes to the missing support for the overlay mode.

In the above example, the end format is 692x340 pixels. Neither number can be cleanly divided by 16; some additional work is therefore necessary.

Selecting the correct end size

Put your notepad and pencil down, for the following calculation tool helps you search for the correct end resolution.

The Advanced Bitrate Calculator: A Swiss pocket knife for DivX

In addition to its most important properties of calculating optimal bitrates for DivX files, the DivX bitrate calculator can also determine the correct end resolution for the film. You can download the tool from http://www.divx.com.

When you start the tool, several different calculation variations are offered. From these, select the *Prop.Calc* mode first.

In the *Prop.Calc* tab, you can first select the picture ratio for the output material. The following info box explains the conventional formats.

7. Reserving space for the essential

The most frequently used formats

The following formats can currently be found in the TV as well as DVD realm:

- The **4:3** format is usually used for regular television broadcasts (TV journals, and so forth.).
- The **16:9** format can be found in various made-for-TV movies.
- The **2.35:1** format is being used with current wide-screen movies.

Tip: Simply measure the width and height of the image material on your screen with a ruler and divide the width by the height. This way, you know which format to use.

The following step-by-step instructions exemplify how a movie recorded from TV can be changed to a professional image format. The values indicated refer only to the present example and can be completely different from yours.

1 Crop the movie's borders as described above. Be liberal when doing so. In the present case, the cropping was done in connection with the deinterlace filter. Make a note of the two resolution values (in this case, 700x426).

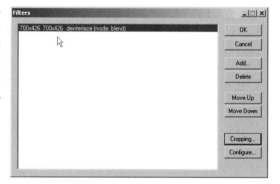

2 Start the Advanced Bitrate Calculator. Use the built-in pocket calculator to establish the ratio of the two resolution values, x/y (in this case 700/426).

3 Go to the *Prop.Calc* tab. Under *Aspect Ratios*, choose the ratio that comes closest to the value calculated in step 2. In the present case, this would be the classic 16:9 ratio.

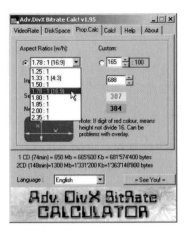

4 Vary the width of the output format (with the *Input width frame* button) until the height of the output format agrees with the green indicator. This way, you have made sure that the height as well as the resolution width is divisible by 16. For the 16:9 format, the final resolution for the example is 512x240 pixels.

Note

Lower the resolution while retaining optimal picture quality

When compressing videos by the DivX process, the selected bitrate is basically responsible for the quality your compressed film has at the end. A lower resolution makes it possible to compress the film at a higher bitrate when encoding. Still, try to also obtain a maximum for the resolution.

5 And now for the last step: Select the *Resize* filter from the *Filter* dialog window and set the values for the filter to the ones calculated in step 4. The results of the rescaling can be displayed in the *Preview* window.

The art of the correct bitrate

In the previous chapters, it has become clear that the bitrate with which movies in DivX format are compressed plays a central role. On the one hand, the quality of the film increases with the bitrate. On the other, the calculated data amount also increases, along with the file size. The goal is to find a compromise for producing a film of the utmost quality that fits on one, or a maximum of two, CDs.

Calculating the movie's bitrate

1 Load the film to be encoded into VirtualDub. Define any necessary filters and, if necessary, crop the borders as described in the previous chapters.

2 Delete any commercial blocks from the raw material. After editing, you can see the remaining time for the entire film at the bottom of the window (in the illustration, 1h 32min 39s).

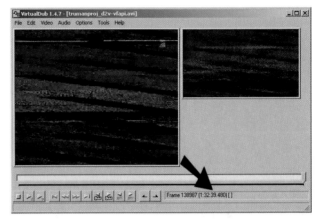

3 Start the Advanced Bitrate Calculator and select the *VideoRate* tab. Depending on your quality requirements, select whether you want to use one CD (lower quality) or 2 CDs (higher quality) under *Input Space*. Select an *Input Sound Rate* of 128 kbps. Important: Be generous when defining the length of the video (in the above case, 95 min, for example). Otherwise, you might be disappointed when, after several hours of encoding, the movie doesn't fit on one CD after all. The program now gives you the recommended bitrate (in this case, 878 kbps).

One or two CDs, that is now the question

Note

As a rule of thumb, 90-minute movies fit onto one CD and are of reasonable quality. If you are dealing with an action film with many fast scenes or your quality requirement is high, it makes more sense to use a higher bitrate and spread the final product over two CDs. You learn how to do this, starting on page 127.

7. Reserving space for the essential

4 It is now time to advise the codec in VirtualDub of the calculated bitrate. Open the codec configuration dialog window by going to *Video/Compression/Configure* and enter the calculated value under *Output video bitstream*. For the bitrate mode, select the first pass of the 2-pass encoding. Also determine the save location for the two-pass log file.

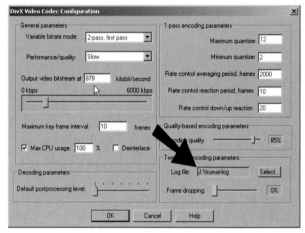

The thing about the key frames – Ensuring smooth playback

Set the *Maximum key frame interval* to a low value (for example, 10 frames). Otherwise, when you play the movie back on a software player later, the movie might not jump to any spot without problems, for the key frames serve as stopping points.

But what is actually the purpose of the two-pass process?

Two-pass encoding for predefined file sizes

The two-pass encoding stays more precisely to the predefined bitrates than the one-pass encoding, so that the end size of your DivX file really does not exceed the previously determined value. This is contingent upon your allowing the first pass to be undertaken in its **entirety**.

And, be careful. The two-pass process also requires double the amount of encoding time of the one-pass process. Decide for yourself if the cost/performance ratio is right for you.

5 Ensure that the video mode is set to *Full processing*. For the audio mode, select *Direct stream copy* because the sound should only be compressed afterwards.

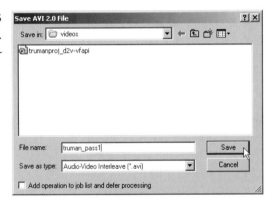

Note

When dealing with video material containing sound, compress the sound after encoding.

If you encode the image and sound data in one shot, you steal valuable computer time from the video processing. Compressing the audio afterwards saves a noticeable amount of time. If you are letting the computer run overnight anyway, you might as well perform the video and audio compression at the same time.

Encoding the video

1 Start the encoding process as usual by going to *File/Save as AVI*. Define the output file with the file-name **pass1*.

2 You should allow the first pass to run completely to comply precisely with the specified bitrate. The second pass that follows requires an exact analysis of the entire movie.

7. Reserving space for the essential

Reuse the log file

Created during the first pass, a film's log file can be used as an analysis file for several encodings (for example, with different bitrates). Then, only each second pass needs to be processed.

3 For the second pass, you need to change the codec configuration. Once again, go to the *Video/Compression* menu, select the DivX codec, and set the *Variable bitrate mode* to *2-pass, second pass*. Make sure that the correct log file from the first pass has been selected.

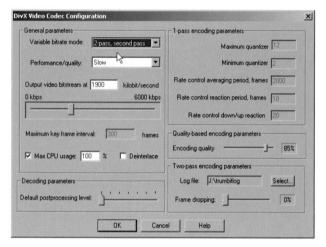

4 Now, save the final file once again by going to *File/Save as AVI*. Define the output file with the filename *pass2*. This becomes the first playable DivX file.

Encode a small section and check the quality

As with the first pass, you can stop the encoding during the second pass at any time with *Abort*. For our ease, VirtualDub creates a video file that can be played back, and whose quality can be checked, before the entire film becomes encoded. This action saves time and nerves in case you have accidentally set one of the parameters incorrectly.

Compressing the sound data

You have probably asked yourself when you looked at the encoded file why, even though compressed, the size is still far from that predicted by the Advanced Bitrate Calculator. The reason is obvious. For the above encoding, the stream copy mode was selected for the audio file, meaning that no compression of the audio file took place. Some editing is necessary here.

1 Load the encoded file into VirtualDub. Set the video mode to *Direct stream copy*. However, set the audio mode to *Full processing*, for the audio data should also be compressed.

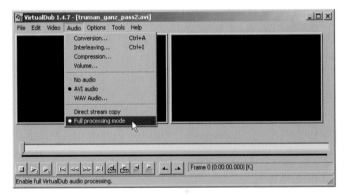

2 In the *Select audio compression* dialog window (go to *Audio/Compression* to reach it), select the MPEG Layer 3 codec with the rate that was indicated for the sound data in the Advance Bitrate Calculator (in our case, 128 kbps).

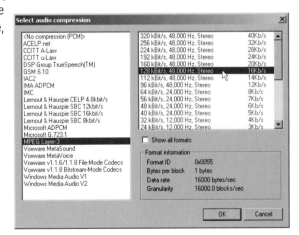

3 Go to *File/Save as AVI* again and save the end file under a new name. Once you've done this, the encoding for the sound data begins. You can see in the progress windows that this proceeds considerably faster than the encoding of the video material (noticeable, among other things, by the higher frames-per-second number). For the audio compression, count on a time span of about one third of the length of the video.

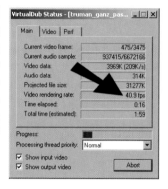

If you have made it to this point and have followed all the instructions step for step, you have every right to describe yourself as a DivX expert. And if you feel driven to greater success, you can do the following:

Expert tool: NanDub

NanDub is a further development from VirtualDub and was especially conceived for the encoding of dynamic bitrates.

The user interface is to a large extent identical to VirtualDub (Filter menu, and so forth); the difference is merely in the selection for the video compression: the SBC (Smart Bitrate Control) item appears there, which is a highly specialized setting designed for dynamic bitrates.

In connection to the "old" DivX 3.11 alpha codec, NanDub keeps considerably closer to the predefined bitrates.

The following images are meant to give you a first impression of NanDub's environment and to invite you to explore it on your own.

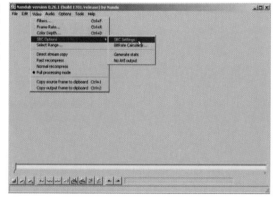

You can download NanDub from http://www.sourceforge.net.

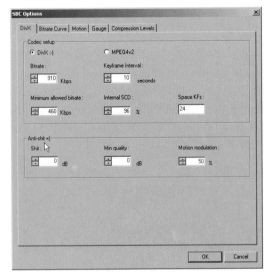

8. Burning DivX videos to CD

Every somewhat experienced computer user who has already burned a CD thinks "I can manage that ..." and wants to skip this chapter. But don't be in such a rush. This chapter also contains additional tips on how you can use every last available bit on the blank CD (keyword "overburning") and how to break up videos precisely (that is, divide them onto two CDs). And to do all that, you do need a bit of know-how.

> **Burning with Nero**
>
> The following explanations refer to the burning program Easy CD Creator. You can download a fully functional trial version at
>
> http://www.roxio.com
>
> All instructions should in effect be transferable from other burning programs (Win OnCD, Feurio, and so forth) without any problems.

Note

The 1-CD project

In the chapter *Reserving space for the essential*, you have created a DivX file that you can now burn to a single CD. To do this, proceed in the following way:

Configuring Easy CD Creator

1 Start the program Easy CD Creator. In the program window, select the option *make a data CD* and then *data CD project*.

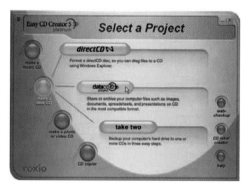

2 Name the CD. In the browser window, select the directory of your choice. Right-click a file in the directory and select *Explore* to view the file.

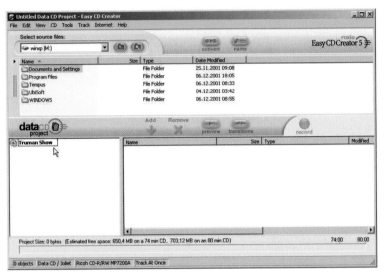

3 Select the DivX file you want to burn to CD. Click *Add* to include the file in your compilation. Don't let the displayed file size disconcert you. The numbers are in bits not bytes.

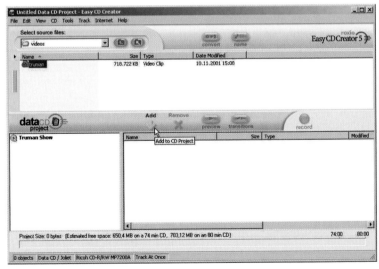

8. Burning DivX videos to CD

As long as the display at the bottom of the screen still shows free space on the medium of your choice, the data fits onto one CD (in this case, of 700 MB) without your resorting to tricks.

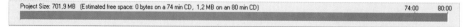

It becomes critical when the display reads *0 MB* (more about that later).

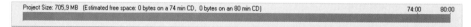

4 Now start the actual burn process by clicking *record*.

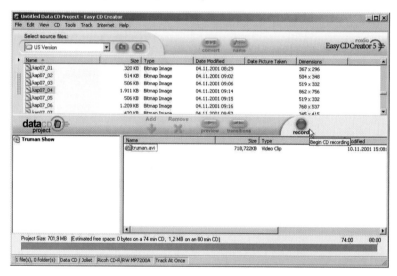

Burning the CD

1 First, set the highest write speed possible and ensure that the *Buffer underrun prevention* option is enabled. Click *Options* to reach further configuration options.

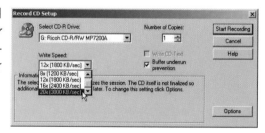

Select the *Finalize CD* option and set the *Record Options* to *Record CD*.

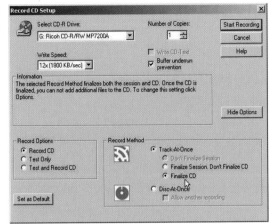

2 Begin the burning process by clicking *Start Recording*. During the actual burning process, a status window displays the writing progress. With a modern burner (for example, 20x CD-R), the entire thing should take less than 5 minutes.

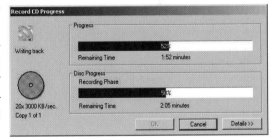

3 With the help of Windows Explorer, check to see if the file was burned to the CD correctly; then enjoy your first movie "hot off the press".

Endowing your CD with Autorun

With a little trick, your CD starts automatically as soon as it is inserted. To accomplish this, you only need to use the Windows autorun function:

1 Use any editor to create a file containing the following:

```
[autorun]
open=start wmplayer.exe /play /close \file name.avi
```

Ensure that the filenames and paths match.

2 Save the file under the name *autorun.inf* and, in Easy CD Creator, copy it to the same folder as the files that are to be burned to CD.

Do you want more room? Overburning blank CDs

Nothing is more frustrating than finding out, after a long-winded encoding process, that the codec didn't quite stick to the file size pre-calculated by the Advanced Bitrate Calculator. Often, it is only a few MBs that induce the burning program to display the despised red bar indicating the capacity has been exceeded.

> **Overburning is risky for older burners!**
>
> At this time, it should be pointed out that the process of overburning should only be undertaken with recently manufactured burners. There is a danger of damaging the hardware, because, in some cases, the laser is forced to regions that it could not normally reach during normal operation.
>
> There is no guarantee that overburning with certain writers and certain media types functions reliably.

Generally, you can assume that most blank CDs allow you to overshoot the capacity by several MBs. The manufacturers naturally do not disclose what the limits of this tolerance are, so you are required to experiment. The following instructions show the best way of proceeding.

> **The right overburning software: Nero**
>
> Easy CD Creator does not tolerate overburning. For this process, you need the software Nero Burning ROM. You can download a trial version of the program from
>
> http://www.nero.com

The basic setup of the program is similar to that of Easy CD Creator. Thus, in the following, we only discuss the details of the overburning process.

1 Open Nero and select the *CD-ROM (ISO)* project. Make sure to enable the option *No Multisession*. Compile your video files by dragging and dropping them as you would in Easy CD Creator. In the following ex-
ample, assume that the
CD capacity has been ex-
ceeded by very little. You
can recognize this by the
red marking on the status
bar.

2 The first thing you need to do is to determine by how much the maximum capacity is being overshot. To do this, go to *File/Preferences* and change the time of the red marker under *Status bar*. Confirm with *Apply* and check the result. Repeat this procedure until the red indicator for overshooting the time has disappeared from the *Status bar*. Make a note of the corresponding value (in the present case, an over-capacity of 15 seconds should be assigned to the 80-min CD).

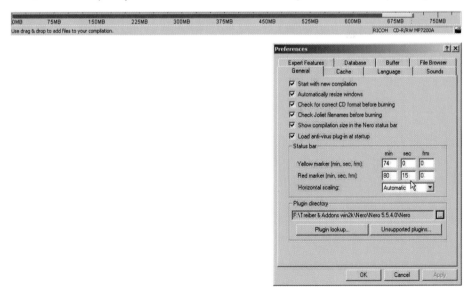

8. Burning DivX videos to CD

3 Click the *Expert Features* tab. Select *Enable overburn disc at once burning* and enter the time you determined in step 2 for the *Maximum CD length*.

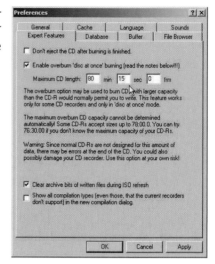

4 Because the overburning process only works in the *Disc at Once* mode, you must enable this mode in the *Burn* tab of the *Write CD* dialog window before the actual burning.

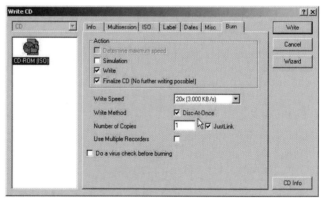

5 Now, it's time to keep your fingers crossed that your writer and the CD-R you are using allow the overburning. Otherwise, it means going back to the beginning and selecting a lower bitrate for encoding.

The 2-CD project

This section is for the perfectionist in you, who wants to cram a movie onto one CD no matter what.

So, you have encoded a film with a relatively high bitrate (calculated using the Advanced Bitrate Calculator), and the end product has to be divided between two CDs. Proceed as follows:

1 Load your encoded video into Virtualdub. Open the *AVI Information* window by going to *File/File information* and make a note of the value given there for the total *# of frames*. Divide this value by two (in the example, this would give 138112 / 2 = 69056).

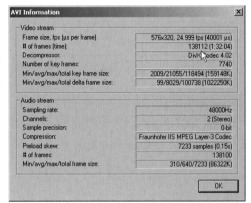

2 Go to the calculated frame by following *Edit/Go to* (or, optionally, by pressing Ctrl+G).

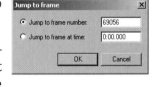

3 Use the key frame keys to search for a scene transition in the vicinity of this frame. With *Mark in*, select the beginning of the region to be cut and make a note of the number of the frame found there (in this case, 69008).

4 Go to the end of the movie and select the end of the region to be cut. Press (Delete) to delete the selected region (approximately half the movie).

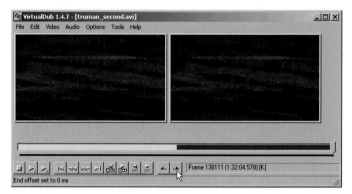

5 Make sure that the video as well as the audio processing is set to *Direct stream copy*. Save the first part of the movie by going to *File/Save as AVI*.

6 Re-open the entire film in VirtualDub. Now, select the region from the beginning of the film to the key frame selected in step 3 and cut the first part out. Save the second part by going to *File/Save as AVI*.

Each part is then burned onto the CD separately, as described in the section *The 1-CD project*.

You have now met the requirements for enjoying portable movies of the highest quality.

9. DivX movies on the computer, TV, and so forth

In this chapter, you learn how to use your painstakingly created DivX material as imagined; namely as a space-saving video-preserve for an enjoyable evening at home in front of the computer or TV, or for when you're traveling with your laptop or PDA.

Optimal playback of DivX movies on your computer monitor

Selecting the right software player

The DivX software player used until now, *The Playa*, which is part of the DivX Bundle, functions well but lacks the convenience to which you are used with a software DVD player, for example.

As the first candidate for offering a convenient DivX environment, the MicroDVD player deserves a closer look.

> **DivX movies with a DVD feel: The MicroDVD player**
>
> The name is somewhat misleading. You are not dealing with a member of the software DVD player category. "MicroDVD" is rather a shortening for the DivX CDs you can play with the software, but the name is not entirely inappropriate, either.
>
> MicroDVD is a shareware program; the registration is $10. The functionality of the unregistered version of the program is restricted.
>
> At the time of printing, the distribution system for the program was in an upheaval, so the best way to find the software is through a search engine.

After you install and start the program, a console that strongly resembles the style of such programs as PowerDVD opens.

9. DivX movies on the computer, TV, and so forth

When playing back a DivX movie, first ensure that the player is in *MicroDVD* mode (visible by the faintly highlighted white *M*). Use *F* to conveniently switch back and forth between the *MicroDVD* mode and the *File* mode (in which you display the videos contained on the hard drive).

After you have pressed *Play*, a window opens where you can select the file to play. Go to *File* and indicate the location of the file to be played back. Confirm your choice with *OK*. The movie should now start. In the adjacent window, you can create "playlists", that is, lists of several films that should be played back in succession.

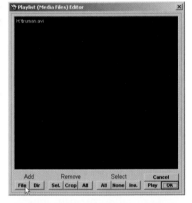

Playing back two films in succession without interruption – the playlist makes it possible

If you have separated a movie into two CDs as directed in the section *Burning DivX videos to CD*, and you have two CD drives at your disposal (for example, one each for a burner and a DVD-ROM), simply put one CD in each of the drives. By defining a corresponding playlist, you can play the two CDs in succession.

Click the configuration button (with the "gear" symbol) to get to the configuration menu for the MicroDVD player.

The menu is divided into several sections. The adjacent section, for example, contains all the settings concerning transparent subtitles. If your graphics card doesn't work in overlay mode, this option should be disabled; otherwise, the program persistently displays error messages during the playback of the movie.

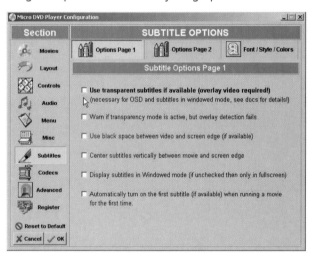

Exploration of the other options is left up to you.

Configuring the hardware correctly

The weakest link in the chain with regard to the playback of DivX videos is the CD-ROM or DVD drive.

> **Note**
>
> **Playing back DivX directly from CD: Enabling DMA or Bus Mastering**
>
> "DMA" stands for "Direct Memory Access" and makes it possible to access PC components such as the CD-ROM drive directly, without the help of the processor. With modern computer systems, Bus Mastering has replaced DMA access.

Enabling Bus Mastering or DMA depends on the system. With Windows 9x, it is enough to just right-click the CD-ROM icon in the window for My Computer to set the DMA directly in the menu.

On a Windows 2000/XP system, it is best to examine the IDE controller in the Device Manager to see if Bus Mastering is enabled.

Double-clicking the components shows the properties of the corresponding IDE channels.

Adjusting the resolution

The resolution of modern computer monitors (for example, 1024x768 pixels for a 17-inch monitor) is generally too fine for the display of video material. In comparison, even modern plasma display televisions only have a maximum resolution of 852x480 pixels (for example, Panasonic plasma display TH-42PW4EX).

Optimal playback of DivX movies on your computer monitor

Notice a considerable increase in the quality of DivX movies when playing them on a computer monitor, but also when playing them on a television, if you reduce the resolution of the player's picture. Proceed in the following way with the MicroDVD player:

1 Open the player's configuration menu. Go to the section *Layout Options* and select the properties page *Display 2*.

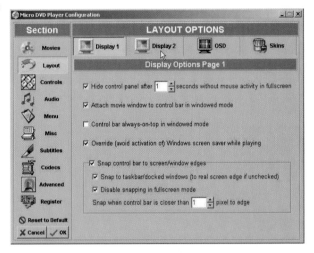

2 First, enable the option *When switching to fullscreen, change screen resolution to* and *Optimal resolution* underneath. Or, simply select the desired resolution manually.

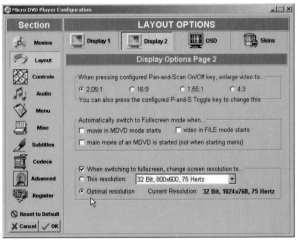

3 Next, start the playback of the movie, switch to *Fullscreen* mode using the *Window/Fullscreen* key (shortcut key (Z)), and enjoy the excellent quality of the image.

When playing back the signal on TV, reduce the resolution to a maximum of 800x600 pixels. More about that in the next chapter.

Outputting the movie to TVs

Expect few cases in which you can convince your friends to gather for a movie night around your computer monitor.

Therefore, it makes more sense to transfer the image signal to a standard television, as explained in the following section.

From PC to TV – Basic wiring

The following illustration shows the necessary physical connections for connecting a TV to a standard graphics card with *TV Out*:

You need:

- A graphics card with a *TV Out* connection. This is usually standard on most graphics cards.
- A junction for the soundcard, which separates the *Speaker Out* into the two stereo channels through Cinch plugs.
- A connection cable that carries the signal to the television.

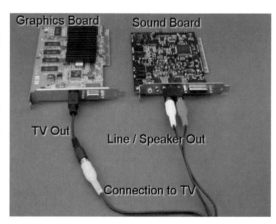

For super sound, connect the Cinch plug to a stereo system

With the connection method described above, it is also possible to connect the two stereo channels using simple extension cables to the AUX input of a standard stereo system. Then it sounds almost like in the movie theater.

On the air tonight – Transferring the TV signal through a wireless transmission

In the age of wireless networks, you no longer need to worry about pulling cables through the house to the television or to the stereo system, or even possibly ripping walls open.

The following illustration shows a simple and affordable solution for transmitting the TV signal using a gigahertz wireless transmitter from the computer to the television:

(Seen at http://www.trust.com/convenience)

The devices illustrated above are also in a position to remotely transmit the infrared signal by wireless means.

Infrared remote control for the computer

In the meantime, several accessories for controlling the computer remotely have also become available.

Conjuring up the image on the television

Many a user has been frustrated trying to conjure up a computer image on the television. The Internet forums are full of desperate calls for help on this subject.

To prevent this from happening to you, use the following instructions.

9. DivX movies on the computer, TV, and so forth

In the next example, a graphics card is configured with the widespread Conexant Bt869 chip for generating the TV signal. You can find out the type of your TV chip by going to the properties tab for the display.

1 Turn on your TV and select the special *AV* channel (identical with channel "3" for many televisions).

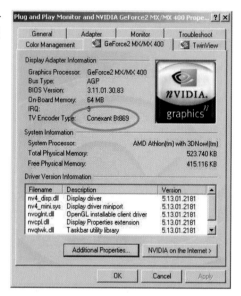

2 You can accomplish the switch by right-clicking the Desktop and selecting the *Properties* option from the open pop-up menu. In the *Display Properties* dialog box, go to the *Settings* tab and click *Advanced.*

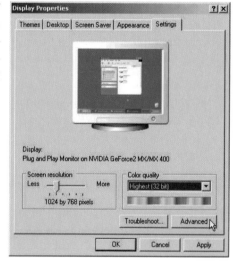

3 Depending on the type of graphics card, select the setting for displaying the desktop image on two monitors from the *Display* list box. (In the illustration, the menu item is called *TwinView*.) Select the corresponding option for displaying the image on the TV (in this example, it's called *Clone*).

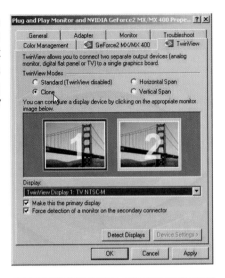

4 Confirm your setting by clicking *Apply*. The warning message that appears must be acknowledged with *OK*. Now, the Desktop image should appear on the TV.

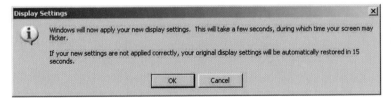

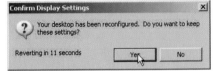

Did it work? Or is your colorful Desktop image black and white on your TV?

An old problem .... Solve it as follows:

Changing black & white to color: From PAL to NTSC

It is standard for most graphics card drivers with the TV Out option to be set to display in the NTSC television standard (which is the norm for the US). If the PAL setting, the norm for Europe, was accidentally set, you can change it by going to the advanced options for the graphics card drivers.

9. DivX movies on the computer, TV, and so forth

In this system configuration (NVidia/Bt869), you can set the NTSC mode under *Select output device* in the TwinView *Device Settings* window, which you can locate over *Device Settings*.

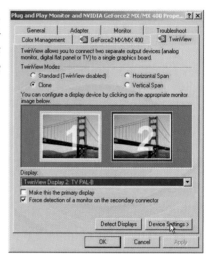

Here, it is also important to select *Composite Video-Out* from the *Video output format* list box, unless you own a television with S-Video capability.

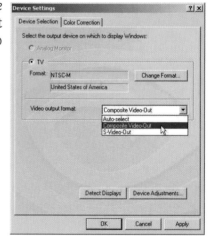

S-Video – the highest quality for transferring the video signal

S-Video stands for Super Video. With the S-Video standard, the video signal is split into a luminance (brightness) and a chrominance (color) signal. The image displayed on the television in this way is sharp and brilliant.

The last thing that needs to be said is that most graphics card manufacturers pay little attention to the *TV Out* connection from a software standpoint. In particular, the problem of adjusting the picture size on the television is usually solved unsatis-factorily. The following section shows how you can use software to reach an optimal TV picture display.

Optimal picture reproduction using TVtool

Note

TVtool

TV Tool can be downloaded as a demo from http://www.tvtool.de/index_e.htm. The unregistered version automatically closes after 10 minutes and TV mode switches off, so you can test the functionality of the program well. Registration and unrestricted use of the software costs $10.

After installation, start TVtool. Make sure that *Dual-View* mode is selected and the picture format is set to *NTSC*. Use the green *TV Mode* button to add the television picture.

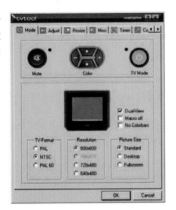

If a color image of the Desktop doesn't appear on the television, select the *Adjust* tab and indicate *VHS* as the *Connection* type.

If you own a television with an *S-Video* input, select *S-VHS* under *Connection*. Also (as seen above) use the *Non-Interlaced* setting to significantly reduce any flickering.

9. DivX movies on the computer, TV, and so forth

Finally, enjoy your Desktop display in all its glory on the television.

Note

Testing with a portable TV saves running around

If possible, do the first tests with the TV Out of your graphics card with a TV near the computer. Portable devices are particularly well suited for this, unless you want to jog to the living room to test every little setting.

Tvtool's options

The following table gives you a short overview of the settings available in each of the tabs.

Tab	Settings
Mode	Select the resolution/switch to TV mode, select the TV format (NTSC/PAL).
Adjust	Adjust the main image on the television, brightness, color saturation, type of video signal (Composite/S-Video).
Resize	Adjust the display of the active window on the TV.
Misc	Settings for various sound options
Timer	Switch off the television signal after a specified time.
Config	Assign keyboard shortcuts for TVtools (call up with the Ctrl+function key).
Info	Contains registration information among other things.

The default functions assigned to the function keys, in combination with the Ctrl key, are as follows:

Function key	Effect
F1	TV mode on
F2	TV mode off
F3	Bring TVtool to the foreground
F4	Start pre-defined program (for example, software DVD player)
F5	Monitor standby mode
F6	Switch to Resize mode for individual windows
F7	Zoom mode for current window

Displaying a window so it fills the TV screen

Using the following instructions, you can fit the MicroDVD player's output window to the television screen. Proceed as follows:

1 Start TVtool. In the *Mode* tab, select the resolution *800x600*, as well as *Fullscreen* mode for the *Picture Size*. Use the green button to switch to *TV* mode. The Desktop should appear on the television screen.

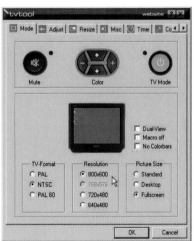

2 In the *Config* tab, select the option *Trayicon enable* to make regular access to the tool through the taskbar possible.

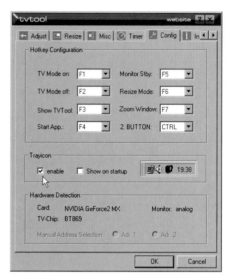

3 In the *Resize* tab, select the options *Show Borders*, *Hide Taskbar,* and *Use Toolbar*. The settings are important for convenient configuration in full screen mode.

4 Then start the DivX application of your choice (in the present example, this is the MicroDVD player). Play back a movie in *Fullscreen* mode in the player window on the computer (the Z key in the MicroDVD player).

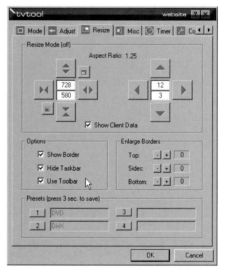

5 Use the shortcut Ctrl+F6 to open the *Resize* window. You can now use the control keys in the *Resize* toolbar to conveniently adjust the size and position of the TV image.

The size adjustment can also be done in the main window of TVtools. Furthermore, you have the possibility of defining 4 different presets (for example, for various movie formats). If you press one of the preset buttons for 3 seconds, you can save the settings you have made under the name of your choice.

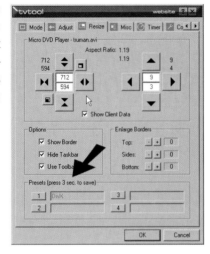

Finally, your DivX movie should be displayed in good quality on your television.

Note

The optimal resolution for DivX: 768x480

See if your graphics card supports the resolution 768x480 for reproduction on a TV. This way, you can save yourself a lot of big adjustments with Tvtool, because this resolution is optimal for playing back DVDs and DivX movies on the television.

Obtaining the above resolution for television sets is often only possible with special graphics card drivers. It is especially necessary to adapt the drivers under Windows 2000/XP to this end.

DivX becomes mobile – Underway with a laptop

In this last section, we want to quickly address some special issues with respect to portable DivX play devices.

Viewing DivX on a laptop

There's nothing easier than viewing DivX on a laptop: Install the software player, insert the movie CD, press play, and go.

It becomes a little trickier if you want to output everything on a television in reasonable quality; a little more manual labor is then required.

From laptop to television

The following description refers to connecting a laptop with an ATI Rage Mobility graphics card to a television.

1 Connect the already familiar SCART adapter cable to the *Video Out* by means of a Cinch plug to the headphone output of the laptop. Connect the SCART plug to the television's inputs as described in the section *From PC to TV*.

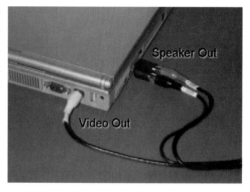

2 On the laptop screen, right-click to open the *Properties* window for the display and, once there, select *Advanced*. There is usually another option, *Display*, with which you can switch to *TV* display. Your Desktop should then appear on the television.

Note

No sound? Turn up the volume on the laptop.

If there's no sound coming from the television, turn on the volume controls. After all, you are using the adjustable headphone output.

3 If you also have problems displaying color, double-click *TV* to open another dialog window, from which you can select the NTSC system as usual.

The rest proceeds as usual, and you can turn the hotel TV into a movie theatre in no time.

9. DivX movies on the computer, TV, and so forth

Also possible: DivX on the PDA

Personal Digital Assistants (PDAs for short) are up and coming. The first playback programs for DivX movies were already spotted on the scene. But do not expect too much (yet); after all, the current memory capacity of 64 MB for such devices is not large. However, if you own such a device, it's certainly worth giving it a try!

10. Surround sound – AC3 and Dolby Digital

Who hasn't at one point or another dreamed of turning the computer into a movie landscape with all the bells and whistles, including the optimal reproduction of sound. The latter requires transforming the PC into a surround sound system – with the possibility of playing back sound in Dolby Digital.

Note

A brief overview of surround sound systems

Dolby Surround (or Dolby 2.0): Transfer of information contained in the 4 channels to two standard stereo channels through a technical trick, the phase shift.

Dolby Digital (AC3 or Dolby 5.1): Transfer of the sound signal over 5 full sound channels (front left, front center, front right, back left, and back right) and one bass channel (therefore 5.1).

DTS and THX: No surround sound system, but quality levels of the audio signal.

With the help of the AC3 sound signal, you can use 6 loudspeakers, provided you have a suitable soundcard. In theory you have three possibilities for retrieving the AC3 sound components from the computer:

- Outputting over a SPDIF digital output to the AC3-capable amplifier of a stereo system.

- Outputting directly through a Dolby 5.1-capable soundcard connected to a group of speakers.

- Outputting the AC3 sound information over a software converter directly to the speakers on the computer. It is self-evident that this variation only serves the purpose of testing, for it does not lead to the enjoyment of surround sound.

The following tutorial is concerned with the creation of DivX movies with AC3 sound.

Extracting AC3

First you learn how to extract the AC3 stream from a DVD with the help of SmartRipper. Proceed as follows:

1 Insert a DVD with AC3 sound (this has become the standard) and start Smart Ripper. In *Movie* mode, select the chapter of your choice (or, optionally, the entire movie; see page 12). Then, go to the *Stream Processing* tab.

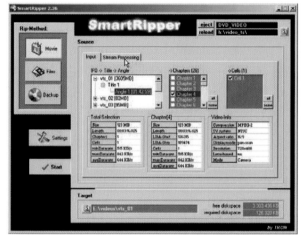

2 Select *Enable Stream Processing* and first choose the video stream. Select *Direct stream copy* as the video stream option. In addition, click the sound track of your choice. A corresponding notation informs you if you are dealing with an AC3 sound track.

3 Select the sound track and enable the option *Demux to extra file*. Have a look at the output path under *Target*. This is where the AC3 stream is saved.

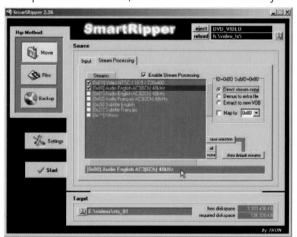

4 Start the usual ripping process with *Start*. The program extracts the VOB file as well as separates the AC3 stream. Keep track of the output in Windows Explorer.

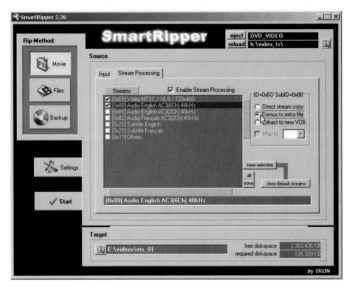

The *.ac3 audio file obtained in this way can no longer be played back using standard software. The file can, however, be examined using BSPlayer (see page 131).

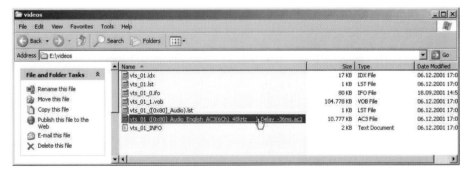

Retrieving AC3 from a satellite signal

AC3 by satellite

More and more television stations are transmitting the Dolby Digital signal by satellite. If you own a DVB card, you can create your own DivX CDs with AC3 sound.

Retrieving the AC3 signal from a satellite signal differs somewhat from the extraction from a DVD and is formally and completely explained in the following.

Ensure that your DVB software allows for the recording of AC3 Mpegs. WinDVB Live2000 has proven itself in this respect and can be downloaded from http://www.odsoft.org.

1 Start your DVB software and go to the configuration tab for recording.

2 Set the file type as MPGAC3. This combines the Mpeg2 video stream with the AC3 audio stream.

3 Open the program DVD2AVI (compare to page 58 and load the program to be edited by going to *File/Open*.

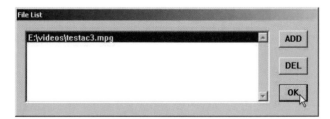

4 In the *Audio* menu, ensure that the option *Channel Format* is set to *Dolby Digital*, and that in the *Dolby Digital* menu, *Demux all tracks* was selected as well.

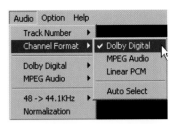

The option *Dolby Surround Downmix* is also of interest here. It makes the conversion from the 6-channel information to the normal two stereo channels possible. That shouldn't occur here, of course.

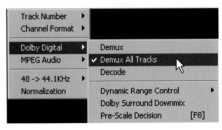

5 You can start the Demux process by going to *File/Save Project*.

Combining video and sound with NanDub

After you have successfully extracted the sound information from the DVD or the satellite signal, you should convert the video into DivX format as already described in several sections of this book. This is done the usual way with VirtualDub.

You should trouble yourself with one more tool, solely for the combining of the AC3 stream: NanDub, the software mentioned on 118. Start the program and proceed as follows:

10. Surround sound – AC3 and Dolby Digital

1 Load the movie material that was encoded with VirtualDub into NanDub by going to *File/Open video file*. Make sure that both the video and the audio *Direct stream copy* options are enabled.

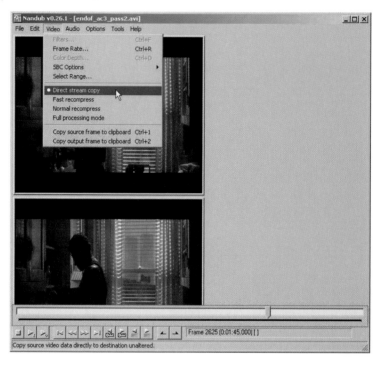

2 In the *Audio* menu, click *AC3 audio*. In the Explorer window that opens, select the AC3 file and confirm your selection with *Open*.

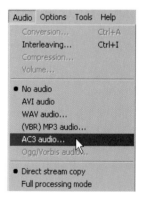

A window should open that shows the correct transfer of the file.

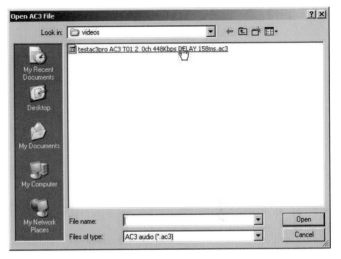

3 In the *Audio/Video Interleave Options* dialog window, select *Enable audio/video interleaving* and enter the delay value, which you can read from the name of the AC3 file.

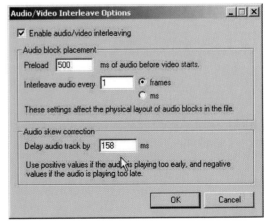

4 Finally, to avoid synchronization problems: from the *Video* menu, select the *Video frame rate control* menu item. In the dialog box, select the option *Change so video and audio durations match* in the *Frame rate conversion* category.

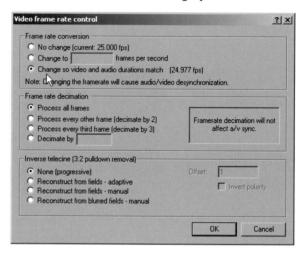

That's it – all you have to do now is go to *File/Save as AVI* and the AC3 movie is finished.

Open the movie immediately in a player. You most likely hear ... nothing!

You learn how you can get your mini movie theatre to sound right in the next section.

Making AC3 sound audible

AC3 – The right player does it

Only a few DivX software players are equipped with the necessary tools to play back AC3 sound. One of these is the PowerDivX player. You can download it from

http://www.blacksunsoft.fr.st

After installation and once you've started the program, the following image appears:

By pressing *Config*, the following configuration dialog window opens:

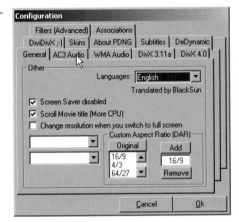

In this case, the *AC3 Audio* tab is of particular interest. Selecting this tab displays the following window:

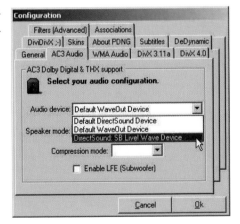

From the *Audio device* list box, you can select your sound output device. You have a choice between the Windows DirectSound components (contained in the DirectX package) or the hardware-specific driver.

Choose a *Speaker mode* from the list box according to your speaker configuration.

10. Surround sound – AC3 and Dolby Digital

Naturally, the *6 Speakers Mode* would be the crowning glory; you could then create a true Dolby Digital 5.1 environment.

But the *SPDIF Output* is also interesting. It produces a digital output of the signal to an AC3-capable receiver/amplifier, using the corresponding output on the soundcard.

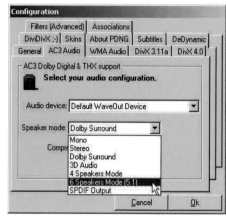

Feel free to experiment with the various sound configurations and find the one that's optimal for you. You are rewarded by the output of a true, rich sound tapestry.

Also worth mentioning is that the installation of the PowerDivX player is accompanied by the following side effect:

PowerDivX is installed, and Media Player can also be used

Once PowerDivX has been installed, MS Media Player and other software DivX players come alive with AC3 sound – apparently the PowerDivX package contains special AC3 drivers that are recognized by the entire Windows system.

Index

Index

Index

W